The Real Food Cook Book

Nutritious & delicious dishes for the whole family to enjoy

In good health
Ellen x

Ellen Picton
Zoë Harcombe

Published by Columbus Publishing Ltd 2016

www.columbuspublishing.co.uk

ISBN 978-1-907797-55-2

Version 20161127

A CIP record of this book is available from the British Library.

Cover design by Andy Harcombe

Typesetting and design by Raffaele Bolelli Gallevi

The content of this book is intended to inform, entertain and provoke your thinking. This is not intended as medical advice. It may, however, make you question current medical and nutritional advice. That's your choice. It's your life and health in your hands.

Neither the author nor the publisher can be held responsible or liable for any loss or claim arising from the use, or misuse, of the content of this book.

Acknowledgements

I must start by thanking Zoë and Andy Harcombe for supporting this project, without them this book would not be possible.

I am dedicating this book to my Grandfather, Ceri Parry, who always gave me words of wisdom and encouragement. He gave me many recipe books and wrote messages in each. My favourite says: 'To the queen of cuisine on your 17th birthday, keep cooking – good looking'. And so I did.

I must thank my husband, Anthony, for all his support, for listening to all of my recipe ideas, and for giving feedback on new dishes but most importantly, for cleaning the pans that don't fit in the dishwasher.

I hope that when my daughter, Isabelle, is older she will love cooking as I do.

Ellen Picton

Contents

Introduction
(By Zoë)

Ellen is an incredible person with an incredible personal health story. Aged 19, she was diagnosed with Coeliac disease. The prescription for gluten-free (fake) foods stimulated Ellen's interested in nutrition and real food for two reasons i) because the gluten-free fabrications made her feel so unwell and ii) because they tasted so bad!

Ellen's next health diagnosis was even more upsetting and potentially life changing: in her early 20s she started to suffer with disabling endometriosis. She spent most days strapped to a tens machine and was downing a cocktail of anti-inflammatory drugs in tandem. After several operations, which tried to resolve the endometriosis, Ellen was given the unimaginable choice of having a hysterectomy or being put on a drug to induce the menopause. She was only 24 years old. Ellen was told that she couldn't have children due to the extent of the scar tissue in her womb. Having just met her now husband, Anthony, she had to break the news to him that children wouldn't be part of the package. Thankfully he thought that Ellen was more than enough ☺

While still in shock at the no-children news, Ellen declined both stark medical choices (hysterectomy or menopause) and set out to see how healthy she could become with lifestyle changes. She tried to optimise her nutrition intake, dropped full time work to part time, took up yoga and enjoyed daily walks. Within six weeks of starting the 'healthy-me plan', Ellen then enjoyed the shock of her life – a pregnancy!

The doctors were equally shocked and were convinced that the baby wouldn't make it to term. But "Isabelle" liked being inside Ellen so much, she arrived two week's late. A perfect, healthy baby – or, as Ellen and Anthony describe her "their miracle baby".

Following Isabelle's arrival, Ellen knew that her heart and calling lay in food and nutrition. She took a diploma in nutrition and set up her company "Healthaspire" in Milford Haven Marina – a more natural and inspirational setting would be difficult to find. The premises have a fully accredited cooking demonstration and education facility and two consultation rooms for private consultations.

Ellen was introduced to The Harcombe Diet® by a friend, who had lost weight and managed her own endometriosis by following the plan. Ellen tried the five day Phase 1 and felt great and wished she'd discovered me sooner to avoid years of unnecessary yo-yo dieting (I wish I'd discovered it sooner for the same reason! But then I'd never know what everyone is going through...)

Ellen was looking for a real food, healthy eating plan to adopt at "Healthaspire" and was keen to see if The Harcombe Diet® could be shared in this way. She thought the company was American and so was delighted to hear another Welsh voice at the end of the phone when she tracked us down and spoke to my husband, Andy. We were exploring the possibility of running local clubs at the time and so we were delighted to have the opportunity to help Ellen to run some sessions, to see how the concept would work. The local results were amazing: most people lost 30lbs (15kg) and cured so many ailments alongside.

Ellen has been running weekly groups since January 2015 and has seen hundreds of members lose amazing amounts of weight. She makes the classes unique by discussing a new nutrition topic at each one, or doing a cooking demonstration. Ellen also offers 1-1 private weight loss coaching for people who want something more personal and Skype sessions too, for those further away – even Spain! Ellen is pleased to observe that The Harcombe Diet® delivers what it promises, which is to 'Lose weight and Gain health!'

I have personally presented in Ellen's demonstration room to her club members, with the sun setting over the sea and the seagulls squawking all around. After the talk, over drinks and Harcombe friendly nibbles, I've heard so many wonderful success stories from the regulars: life changing weight loss; diabetes under control and all sorts of digestive problems resolved with real food and Ellen's help.

On one occasion, Ellen hired the local theatre, so that 100 real foodies could come along to hear me speak and sample Ellen's tasty recipes.

It is not an overstatement to say that Ellen is, pretty much single handed, making a difference to the health of Pembrokeshire. In addition to the local clubs, Ellen runs cooking lessons for adults and children, to help them to prepare simple meals from scratch. She has been invited to do cooking demonstrations at food and fish festivals – well, Pembrokeshire is known for the latter! Such is the enthusiasm that Ellen has for cooking and such is the impact that her sessions have, Milford Fish Docks, part of the Port of Milford Haven, have generously sponsored numerous local children to attend cookery courses. Ellen's demonstration record is teaching 140 children to make tuna paté and healthy chocolate treats at a local food festival.

A local private school approached Ellen to ask for help with their school menu and Ellen inspired them to go for a 'refined sugar-free' meal plan. The parents and teachers have been as important as the school chef in achieving this stretch target. The parents and teachers are the ones who should benefit from better behaviour and concentration from the 'stable energy' children. Ellen is now a master at hiding vegetables in everyday foods, although children are more inclined to like sweet carrots etc anyway, when they don't have artificial sweetness in their diet.

Healthy eating really has changed Ellen's life and may have played a part in creating another life – Isabelle! It's now her vocation, her passion and her way of keeping her own health conditions under control. Her joy at helping others to be slimmer and healthier is clear to see. This book is Ellen's way of sharing some of the dishes that she cooks – whether in the home kitchen, the business demo area or at food festivals. Enjoy!

Dr. Zoë Harcombe, PhD

Why The Real Food Cook Book? (By Ellen)

The working title for this book was "Freefrom?", before we settled upon "The Real Food Cook Book." All the recipes are gluten-free and most are dairy-free and sugar-free. On the rare occasions that milk is used as an ingredient, other dairy-free options are suggested. Sugar, as in sucrose/table sugar, won't be listed anywhere (other than to look out for sugar in bought ingredients to avoid it!) However, there is some sucrose in the very dark chocolate used in some puddings and dried fruit features in a couple of desserts and honey/maple syrup in one. Hence, we won't claim that the whole book is dairy-free and sugar-free, but the majority of recipes are free from things that you may need/choose to avoid. This will be a great addition to your "Freefrom" recipe repertoire, depending on what you and your family personally want to avoid.

When I was 19 I was diagnosed with Coeliac disease. Coeliac disease is an autoimmune condition. This is where the immune system mistakenly attacks healthy tissue. There is no real cure, apart from removing gluten from the diet.

At the time I was offered a prescription for gluten-free goods, but I did not want to eat all of the processed alternatives. I have always loved cooking, so I enjoyed the new challenge of recreating my favourite recipes to make them naturally gluten-free.

A few years later I became lactose intolerant, so again this meant I had to play around with alternative ideas. Discovering The Harcombe Diet®, I had to give up sugar too! I thought life without gluten, dairy and sugar would be hard. People often ask me, "What exactly do you eat?" This recipe book holds the answers and I hope it helps to inspire you as much as it has done me.

The Harcombe Diet® has helped me to maintain a weight loss of three stone and it has stopped me feeling the depths of despair of yo-yo dieting. It's perfect for me as it naturally excludes all the foods that cause me problems and fits alternatives into a lifestyle that I can live with and enjoy. It most certainly did what it promised, which was to help me to lose weight and gain health!

Food intolerance is becoming more common and many people are having problems, mainly with gluten, wheat and dairy. The 'Freefrom' sections in supermarkets are growing by the minute. The key issue is – just because it's gluten-free, doesn't mean it's healthy. The moral of the story is – eat real food.

These recipes help me to feel that I'm not deprived of anything. They make meals that I eat on a daily basis and they work for all of my family, which includes a hungry husband, an active four year old, and two dogs that eat real food too.

I dislike bland food and Freefrom food shouldn't mean you have to sacrifice on taste. This recipe book should give you lots of 'Freefrom' ideas, which are bursting full of flavour.

A large number of the recipes in this book are also Freefrom meat and fish and are therefore suitable for vegetarians. We've marked these with (V) in the title of each recipe.

Ellen Picton

Stocking Your Larder

Having a well stocked store cupboard in your kitchen really does help when you are trying to throw something together. At first it may seem expensive to buy all of these things, but once you have them they seem to last forever.

I have an entire cupboard and spice rack dedicated to flavour; I love how a few sprinkles of this and that can make such a huge difference to a dish.

Herbs

Dried herbs are really helpful, my favourites include parsley, oregano and rosemary. If you do buy fresh herbs then put any left-over's in the freezer. Then, when you need them, you can crumble them into your cooking pot; they taste just as good as they would fresh.

Top tip – DO NOT throw away the stalks of coriander and parsley – this is a common kitchen mistake – all of the herb has flavour!

Spices

Unless you have a spice grinder, get ground spices. Garam masala is a really helpful one as it's a blend of Indian spices, which makes an instant curry powder. It usually doesn't contain chilli, so you can add flavour without heat.

Dried chilli powder, cumin and coriander, along with turmeric, are also on my spice rack. You can choose garlic powder too, although I must admit I'm a lover of fresh.

Fats

Fat is absolutely essential for the human body. There are good and bad fats. Avoid sunflower and oils high in polyunsaturated fat. They are highly processed and not as healthy as they sound. Stick with cold pressed oils such as olive oil. Use an extra virgin olive oil for salad dressing and a cheaper version for frying.

Coconut oil has become very popular lately It's really versatile and is naturally stable at high temperatures, making it ideal for frying, roasting, adding to soups or baking.

I also use coconut oil to take my make up off and as a moisturiser - just make sure you have one pot for the bathroom and one for the kitchen!

Butter, lard and beef dripping are also natural. One of my favourite side dishes is onions fried in beef dripping – try to make celeriac roasties with it, add some salt – and potatoes will soon be a thing of the past!

Vinegar

Raw apple cider vinegar and balsamic are great for salad dressings.

Stock Cubes

Check they don't contain wheat as many do, I tend to use a yeast-free stock powder.

Gluten-free soy sauce – Tamari – a little bit goes a long way

Thickeners

Arrow root, corn flour or ground almonds are all good Freefrom substitutes.

Red and White Wine

It's always worth having a bottle of red and white in the house, as there are a number of recipes that are really enhanced by wine. Red wine goes well with tomato, for example – as the French and Italians know well.

2 FOR £3
ROYAL WELSH SHOW
2015
GOLD

Shopping for Real Food

Once you get into shopping for 'real food' then your supermarket visit is so much quicker, as there are only a few aisles that you need to visit.

Try to avoid Freefrom shelves in supermarkets, as they are highly processed. If you are tempted by something processed then read the ingredients and if you don't recognise something then don't eat it!

Here are my top tips for real food shopping:

1) Where possible – buy local

Most Fridays you will find my sausage dog Martha and I at the local Farmers' market. It's one of the highlights of the week. I love trying new produce and Martha gets lots of treats too.

By shopping locally it means you eat seasonally and you support the local economy too – win win all round!

2) Try something new

The great thing about buying local is that you are usually buying from the grower or producer themselves, so if there is something you are unsure of then ask.

You will usually get lots of ideas about how to cook or serve the dish.

3) Do you really need it?

I like to think if it's not for sale at the Farmers market then do I really need it?

You will usually find meats, fish, eggs, vegetables, fruit, salads, cheeses, cream, butter, milk and local honey, which is more than enough to stop you from going hungry.

4) Buy the best you can afford

Try to buy organic or outdoor bred meat, wild fish and free range eggs along with the most local and fresh vegetables you can get your hands on.

If you feel that eating this way is expensive then remind yourself how much a takeaway meal would be – plus your body is the only place you have to live, so it's worth the investment, after all – food is medicine!

5) Avoid temptation

If you are someone who is easily tempted by packets and marketing ploys then you can try to shop online. Also make sure you don't visit the supermarket when you are hungry.

Tips to Make Cooking Fun and Easy

1) Bulk cook

Every time I cook I always make more than I need, then freeze some.

2) Music

Play your favourite tunes. If you don't like to cook this is a great way to pass the time.

3) Try something new

We all get stuck in a rut and eat the same things. Open this recipe book and pick something out that you haven't tried before and give it a go.

4) Invite friends over

When you cook for guests you make more effort, so invite friends and family for dinner, but make sure they invite you back!

5) Keep it simple

Every night doesn't have to be a gourmet banquet. Save the more complicated dishes for the weekend, plus it gives you something to look forward to.

6) Involve the family

This can create more mess, but it's good for children to learn from an early age about food and where it comes from, and how it's cooked.

Breakfasts

Breakfast is the most important meal of the day – or is it?

This is such a hotly debated topic and personally I feel that the choice of food is more important than the time of day it's eaten.

Remember you are breaking a fast (Break - fast) so if you don't feel hungry, or don't class yourself as a breakfast person, you don't have to eat. The last time I checked there wasn't a law about eating breakfast, so do what feels right for your body. If you want to eat later then you can make something up to have on the run, or, at the weekend, hold off until brunch.

If you wake up hungry and love breakfast then start by avoiding commercial cereals and wheat based breakfasts like toast – even worse – toast with margarine. Choose something natural instead.

When we wake up, our blood sugar levels are usually balanced, so starting the day with protein, along with healthy fat, will help to keep them that way. It will also help you fuller for longer. If something cooked doesn't take your fancy then overnight oats or my 'meal in a glass' smoothie would be a good choice.

I understand that time can be tricky in the morning – especially if you are like me and have a school lunch box to get ready, dogs to feed and breakfast to prepare for yourself.

I tend to make things up in bulk: a large omelette that can be kept in the fridge for a few days; or I cook bacon in batches and chop it up over scrambled egg; and I make up the granola or overnight oats to have with berries.

Going continental can be a quick choice too: such as cheeses and cold meat slices or some fresh fruit.

You will find lots of lovely ideas to inspire you in this section of the book.

Baked Porridge (V)

- Serves 4
- Phase 2

Ingredients

150g oats

1 tsp cinnamon

1/2 tsp ground nutmeg

2 bananas, chopped

500ml milk of your choice

1 tbsp vanilla essence

100g blueberries

For when you feel like you want something carby, this dish hits the spot. It can also be served as a dessert. This recipe contains cinnamon, which is a great spice for adding natural sweetness. Evidence suggests that it can balance sugar levels, is anti inflammatory and could also help fight bacterial and fungal infections.

Method

1. Preheat the oven to 150°c / 300°f.
2. Mix the oats, spices and bananas together in a bowl.
3. Pour in the milk and vanilla essence, and stir until everything is combined together.
4. Pour the mixture into a Pyrex dish and top with blueberries.
5. Place on the middle shelf of the oven and bake for 35 minutes.
6. Serve warm.

Cook's Note

- If you have a problem with dairy then you can use alternative milks such as unsweetened almond milk.
- If you are following The Harcombe Diet, low fat milk is recommended for carb meals.

Bacon and Egg Muffins

- Serves 4
- Phase 2

Ingredients

1 tbsp olive oil

4 eggs

4 bacon medallions

40g grated cheddar

Pinch cayenne peppe

My daughter calls these muffins 'Bacon cakes', which makes them great for all the family.
They are so simple to make and once cool can be wrapped in foil and used for a lunch box (no matter what your age).

Method

1. Preheat an oven to 175°c / 350°f.
2. Oil 4 compartments of a deep muffin tray.
3. Place one piece of bacon into each of four compartments.
4. Crack each egg over the bacon.
5. Sprinkle with grated cheddar and a pinch of cayenne pepper
6. Place onto the middle shelf of an oven and bake for 20 minutes.
7. Eat warm or leave to cool and store in the fridge.

Cook's Note

- You can leave out the cheddar cheese to make this a simple phase 1 dish.

Baked Breakfast Omelette

- Serves 4/6
- Phase 2

Ingredients

6 gluten-free sausages

2 tbsp olive oil

2 spring onions, chopped

100g cherry tomatoes, halved

100g mushrooms, sliced

250g diced pancetta or bacon lardons

8 eggs

250g full fat soft cheese

100g cheddar, grated

1 tsp dried herbs

This omelette is a one-pan wonder, which contains approximately 20g of protein per slice so it will help to keep you full for hours.

Protein is essential for repairing cells and making new ones and so is vital for the human body. We need approximately 1 gram of protein per kilogram of body weight, so that's between 50g - 80g a day for most of us (more for pregnant women and certain athletes may choose to consume more). This bacon, egg and sausage breakfast in a pan will be a healthy start to any day.

Method

1. Preheat the oven to 175°c / 350°f.
2. Heat the oil in a large non-stick pan.
3. Fry the sausages in the pan until the skins are brown.
4. Add the spring onions, tomatoes, mushrooms, and pancetta into an oiled oven tray or large Pyrex dish.
5. Cut the sausages in half lengthways and place them as evenly as you can over the ingredients on the tray.
6. In a large bowl, whisk the eggs and soft cheese together until you have a pale yellow mixture.
7. Pour the egg mixture into the oven tray to cover the cooked ingredients then top with the cheddar and sprinkle with herbs.
8. Place on the middle shelf of the oven and bake for 35 minutes.

Cook's Note

- Serve hot or leave to cool and store in the fridge for up to 3 days.

Soda Bread (V)

- Makes 1 large loaf
- Phase 3

Ingredients

300g self raising wholemeal gluten-free flour (extra for dusting)

1/2 tsp bicarbonate of soda

50g chilled butter, chopped

1 egg, beaten

25g sunflower seeds (optional)

284ml buttermilk (1 carton)

Soda bread is a traditional Irish loaf, which contains no yeast. This means that it's really quick to make, as it doesn't need to be left to rise. Baker's yeast can also cause abdominal bloating and can feed Candida, so is best kept to a minimum if you have suffered from these conditions.
Bread doesn't often feature in my daily diet, but I am often asked for a gluten-free recipe so here it is.

Method

1. Preheat the oven to 175°c / 350°f.
2. Put the flour and the bicarbonate of soda into a mixing bowl. Then add the butter.
3. Rub the mixture between your fingers until it turns into fine crumbs.
4. Add the egg and sunflower seeds. Stir the mixture thoroughly.
5. Pour in the buttermilk and combine everything to make a thick dough.
6. Turn the dough out onto a floured bread board, or add to a large loaf tin. Sprinkle the dough with flour to prevent sticking and to make it easier to shape into a loaf. You can cut a cross into the top of the dough at this stage.
7. Place the dough onto an oven tray and bake for 30 minutes on the middle shelf of the oven.

Cook's Note

- Leave to cool before slicing.
- Great toasted the next day and served with boiled egg.
- You can vary the recipe by adding grated cheese and spring onions, or olives and sun-dried tomatoes. Use your imagination.

Granola (V)

- Makes approximately 10 servings
- Phase 3

Ingredients

6 tbsp coconut oil

100g unsalted butter

500g oats

2 tsp ground almonds

2 tsp vanilla essence

Commercial granola might look healthy but it often contains lots of hidden sugar. This version is much healthier.

It's handy to have some granola in the store cupboard too, for when you don't have much time. I serve mine with berries and a couple of tablespoons of natural live yoghurt.

Method

1. Preheat the oven to 175°c / 350°f.
2. Put the coconut oil and butter into a large pan. Stir over a medium heat. Once this has melted, turn off the heat.
3. Add the oats to the pan, followed by the ground almonds and vanilla essence.
4. Spread the mixture evenly across an oven tray and bake for 15 minutes on the middle shelf of the oven.
5. Stir the granola thoroughly to make sure it's evenly cooked. You are looking to keep the oats separated, although it is nice when you find a cluster.

Cook's Note

- Leave to cool completely before storing in an airtight container.
- It can be made in batches and keeps for around 7 days in an airtight container.

Broccoli and Stilton Muffins (V)

- Makes 12 muffins
- Phase 2 (without the pine nuts)

Ingredients

1 large onion, peeled and chopped

1 head of broccoli, chopped (grate the stalks)

4 tbsp olive oil (for greasing)

200g stilton cheese

10 eggs

100g pine nuts (optional)

This is a spin on a typical quiche, but without the pastry. The balance of stilton and broccoli gives a wonderful flavour to these muffins. These are ideal for vegetarians too.

It can be difficult for vegetarians to get enough complete protein into their diet, so regularly including eggs and cheese, along with pulses, nuts and seeds will help.

Method

1. Preheat the oven to 175°c / 350°f.
2. Oil the muffin tin with some olive oil and place in the oven to warm up.
3. Add the onion and broccoli to a large mixing bowl.
4. Crumble the cheese in to the onion and broccoli bowl and mix thoroughly.
5. In a separate bowl, whisk together the eggs. Then combine all of the ingredients.
6. Remove the muffin tin from the oven and add two tablespoons of the mixture to each segment. If there is any mixture remaining, top up the muffins equally and sprinkle with pine nuts.
7. Place in the oven for 20 minutes.

Cook's Note

- Serve warm or leave to cool and store in the fridge for up to 3 days.
- Always save the broccoli stalks for soups or stir fry dishes, or grate them into a salad; they contain lots of calcium.

Super Smoothie (V)

- Serves 2
- Phase 3

Ingredients

1 small ripe banana, chopped

1 tbsp sunflower seeds

Handful of kale

100g frozen berries

300ml almond milk

1/2 tsp vanilla essence

This recipe gives you a meal in a glass and is a rich source of a couple of vital nutrients: Sunflower seeds are unbeatable for vitamin E and the kale gives you a good dose of vitamin C.

Method

1. Add the banana, seeds, kale, berries and milk with the vanilla essence into the blender.

2. Blend on the highest setting for 1 minute until the mixture is smooth. Serve immediately.

Cook's Note

- You will need a blender for this recipe.
- As this recipe serves two, you can freeze the leftovers or cover and keep in the fridge for the next day. Just make sure to stir thoroughly before drinking it.
- You can make this Harcombe Phase 2 friendly by leaving out the sunflower seeds. Almond milk is practically water nowadays!

Overnight Oats (V)

- Serves 1
- Phase 2

Ingredients

50g oats

1/2 tsp cinnamon

150g fat free Natural Live Yoghurt

50g blueberries

1 apple, peeled, cored and grated

This recipe can help when you don't have much time in the morning. Make sure you use a 'live' or 'bio' yoghurt as it will contain good bacteria to help keep your gut happy.

Method

1. Mix the oats and cinnamon together in a large mixing bowl, using a large metal spoon.
2. Pour the yoghurt, blueberries, and apple into the mixture and stir together.
3. Place the mixture into a jar or glass and cover with foil. Keep the mixture in the fridge overnight. Breakfast is served.

Cook's Note

- Try using other fruits to add your personal touch.

Tapas

Tapas dishes are great for informal entertaining. These recipes are bursting with flavour and if you find a favourite, it can be served as a bigger portion for a main meal.

Garlic Dough Balls (V)

- Makes 14
- Phase 3

Ingredients

180g ground almonds

100g Parmesan cheese, grated

2 eggs, beaten

250g mozzarella cheese

1 tsp pesto

1/2 tsp garlic powder for the recipe and a bit extra for serving

3 tbsp butter, melted

This dough ball recipe is so more'ish. This was proven when we did the photo shoot for this recipe book and the cameraman ate them all!

Garlic is one of my favourite flavours, it's a wonder food as it is anti-fungal, anti-viral and anti-bacterial. If you feel like you have a cold coming then ramp up the garlic.

Method

1. Preheat the oven to 175°c / 350°f.
2. Add the ground almonds, Parmesan and eggs to a large mixing bowl and stir thoroughly.
3. Shred the mozzarella cheese and mix this in with the other ingredients.
4. Add the pesto and garlic powder.
5. Take a small handful of the dough and shape into 14 balls, roughly the size of golf balls.
6. Place each one on greaseproof paper on an oven tray.
7. Roast for 15 minutes.
8. Spoon the butter over the roasted balls and sprinkle with garlic powder. Serve hot.

Cooks note

- Replace the dry garlic for fresh if you want an extra kick.

Roasted Nuts (V)

- Serves 4 (if you are willing to share)
- Phase 3

Ingredients

100g cashews

100g almonds

50g sunflower seeds

50g sesame seeds

1 tbsp olive oil

1/2 tsp salt

1 tsp chilli powder

If you love savoury snacks, then you will love these crunchy nuts. They can be eaten alone, or sprinkled over a salad.

Method

1. Preheat the oven to 175°c / 350°f.
2. Add all of the nuts and seeds to a large mixing bowl and then pour in the olive oil, salt and chilli powder.
3. Mix all the ingredients with a wooden spoon and spread them evenly across an oven tray.
4. Place the tray into the oven on the highest shelf and roast for 20 minutes.
5. Remove the tray from the oven and use some kitchen towel to wipe off any excess oil.
6. Leave to cool then serve.

Cook's Note

- Store any leftovers in an airtight container.

Prawn and Salmon Roulade

- Serves 4
- Phase 2

Ingredients

250g full fat soft cheese

10 sprigs of chives, finely chopped

1 lemon (for the juice)

250g smoked salmon

1 cucumber, sliced

250g cooked king prawns

Smoked salmon and cream cheese is such a great combination. This recipe is so fresh and full of flavour. There is no cooking involved, so it is really quick and easy to prepare.

Method

1. Put the soft cheese and chives in a mixing bowl.

2. Squeeze the lemon juice into the mixing bowl, making sure that no lemon pips fall into the mixture. Then mix thoroughly with a large metal spoon.

3. Take a piece of smoked salmon and lay it flat on a baking tray. Spread a tablespoon of the mixture over the salmon and roll up to make your roulade. Then slice the roulade into 1cm wide rolls.

Cook's Note

- For tapas, thread a slice of cucumber onto a cocktail stick, then sit the salmon on top and finish with a king prawn.
- Keep in the fridge until ready to serve.

Stuffed Goats Cheese Peppers (V)

- Serves 4
- Phase 2

Ingredients

2 red peppers

2 handfuls of spinach

200g goat's cheese, sliced

1/2 tsp ground nutmeg

This is a perfect vegetarian meal, or it can be used as a side dish to accompany chicken or fish. You can also simply enjoy it alone with a salad.

Method

1. Preheat the oven to 175°c / 350°f.
2. Cut the pepper in half lengthways and scoop out the seeds, then wash them. Try to keep the stalk intact if possible to help retain the pepper's shape.
3. Place the peppers onto an oiled baking tray and stuff each pepper with uncooked spinach.
4. Push equal amounts of the goats cheese into each pepper half.
5. Sprinkle the peppers with nutmeg and then place in the oven for 30 minutes.

Garlic Baked Camembert (V)

- Serves 2
- Phase 2

Ingredients

3 garlic cloves, peeled and halved

Handful of fresh thyme or rosemary

1 whole camembert cheese (in wooden box)

This is what weekend treats are all about: rich creamy and roast garlic to use as a mini fondue all to yourself. You can of course share as part of a tapas table too.

Method

1. Preheat the oven to 175°c / 350°f.
2. Push the garlic cloves into the camembert cheese, until you can no longer see them.
3. Next, push the thyme or rosemary into the camembert cheese. The sprigs should stick out of the top.
4. Bake for 20 minutes.

Cook's Note

- When you cut this, the cheese will melt out – serve immediately.
- This makes a lovely dip or sauce for meat or fish.

Super Sardine Pâté

- Serves 4
- Phase 2

Ingredients

125g unsalted butter, melted

4 x 200g tins of sardines in brine, drained

1 lemon, halved

1 tbsp Italian herbs

Until I made this recipe, I didn't think I liked sardines. It was the thought of crunching through the tiny little bones that put me off, but this method gives you a super smooth pâté that tastes similar to tuna. The tiny bones are the most nutritious part of sardines, so they are important to consume. The bones are especially high in calcium and vitamin D. If you avoid dairy, sardines are an ideal way of getting your bone nutrients.

Method

1. Add the sardines and butter to the food processor.
2. Squeeze all of the lemon juice into the food processor, making sure no lemon pips fall into the mixture.
3. Sprinkle the herbs into the food processor and blend for a few minutes, until you get a smooth paste.
4. Turn out the pâté into an airtight container or ramekin.

Cook's Note

- This can be eaten instantly as a dip or set in the fridge for a few hours for pâté.
- It will stay fresh in the fridge for 3 days or 3 months in the freezer.

Smoked Mackerel Pâté

- Serves 2
- Phase 2

Ingredients

125g smoked mackerel fillets, skinned

50g full fat cream cheese

1 lemon, halved

I do love pâtés, I often make them for lunch and use celery as crudités to scoop up.
This is a recipe that's so easy to make, as there is no cooking involved. It also freezes well so you can make it in batches.

Method

1. Add the smoked mackerel and cream cheese to the food processor.
2. Squeeze the lemon juice into the food processor, ensuring no lemon pips fall in.
3. Blend the mixture together.
4. Once the mixture has blended, transfer to an airtight container and store in the fridge.

Lentil Pâté (V)

- Serves 4
- Phase 2

Ingredients

2 tbsp olive oil

1 onion, peeled and finely diced

200g lentils

150ml boiling water

50g tomato purée

4 tbsp white wine

2 tsp dried herbs

Lentils have such an earthy wholesome taste and make a nice thick pâté. Lentils are also a bit of a 'superfood' in the vegetarian world. They are a useful provider of the B vitamins and especially good for minerals: copper; iron; magnesium; manganese; phosphorus; potassium; selenium and zinc.

Method

1. Heat the olive oil in a large pan.
2. Add the onion to the pan and fry it for a few minutes, until soft.
3. Add the lentils and pour over the boiling water. Allow to simmer on low for around 20 minutes, until the water has been absorbed.
4. Stir in the tomato purée, wine, and herbs.
5. Either add to a blender or mash with a fork.
6. Transfer the pâté to an airtight container and leave to cool before leaving to set in the fridge.

Cook's note

- The wine would strictly make this a Phase 3 dish, but the wine will be simmered off so don't worry about this small cheat.

Pancetta and Chorizo in Red Wine

- Serves 2 as a main meal, or more for a tapas
- Phase 2

Ingredients

1 tbsp olive oil

100g pancetta, diced

200g chorizo, sliced

3 shallots, peeled and finely chopped

4 garlic cloves, finely chopped

2 tbsp tomato purée

2 tbsp smoked paprika

100g black olives (make sure they are pitted)

200ml dry red wine

Pinch of salt

Pinch of pepper

This is one of my favourite meals. The red wine gives it a really rich flavour. I usually enjoy it with a green salad.

Method

1. Heat the olive oil in a frying pan.
2. Add the pancetta and cook for a few minutes, until crispy.
3. Add the chorizo to the pan to fry for a few minutes. The red spices should start to colour the pan.
4. Add the shallots and garlic to the pan. Then leave to sauté for a few minutes.
5. Squeeze in the tomato purée and add the smoked paprika, olives and red wine. Simmer for 20 minutes until the wine evaporates and leaves you with a thicker sauce.
6. Season with salt and pepper. Serve hot.

Cook's Note

- The wine would strictly make this a Phase 3 dish, but the wine will be simmered off so don't worry about this small cheat.

Roasted Chickpeas (V)

- Serves 4
- Phase 2

Ingredients

800g chickpeas, drained

6 tbsp tamari (gluten-free soy sauce)

Chickpeas are full of fibre and nutrients and are especially valuable for vegetarians. These can be eaten alone as a snack or mixed into a salad.

Method

1. Preheat the oven to 175°c / 350°f.
2. Tip the chickpeas onto an oven tray and cover with the tamari.
3. Place in the oven on the highest shelf and bake for 15 minutes.
4. Remove the tray from the oven to give them another stir. Place back in the oven and bake for a further 15 minutes.
5. Leave to cool before serving.

Cook's Note

- You can get gluten-free Tamari sauce without sugar – check the gluten-free part of the supermarket and/or the oriental section. The only ingredients necessary are water, soybeans and salt. If there's anything else that's natural, it's OK. Anything you don't recognise – keep looking for another brand.

Parmesan Chicken Bites

- Serves 4
- Phase 2

Ingredients

500g chicken breast, diced

2 eggs

200g Parmesan cheese, grated

Black pepper

My daughter loves these and thinks they are chicken nuggets, and in a way they are! They are great for all the family and work well with turkey and salmon too.

Method

1. Preheat the oven to 175°c / 350°f.
2. Whisk the eggs together in a bowl and sprinkle the grated Parmesan onto a plate.
3. Using a fork, dip the chicken pieces into the egg mixture, followed by the Parmesan, then place onto a baking tray.
4. Continue the process until all the chicken is covered. Then season with plenty of pepper.
5. Place in the oven and bake for 30 minutes.

Cook's Note

- For a quicker option you can place the chicken pieces into a plastic bag then pour in some of the egg mixture, then the Parmesan, and shake.

Pea, Mint and Feta Salad (V)

- Serves 2
- Phase 2

Ingredients

1 (100g) bag of rocket leaves

1 sweet romaine lettuce

250ml boiling water

100g frozen peas

1 lemon, halved

2 sprigs of mint leaves, chopped

2 tbsp olive oil

100g feta cheese, cubed

These flavours are so fresh and make a perfect summer salad together.

Mint is a great digestive aid: you can use any spare leaves to make up a tea with boiling water and a slice of lemon.

Method

1. Wash and drain the rocket and sweet romaine. Roughly chop the leaves as desired (the rocket may need little chopping, the romaine will need more).

2. Pour the boiling water over the peas and leave them to thaw while you make the dressing.

3. In a mixing bowl, squeeze in the lemon juice, making sure no lemon pips fall in. Add the olive oil and mint leaves and mix thoroughly.

4. Drain the peas and mix the leaves together in a bowl. Pour over the dressing and top with the feta cheese.

Cook's Note

- You can add some grilled chicken or flaked salmon to make this into a main course.

Spicy Belly Pork

- Serves 4
- Phase 2

Ingredients

3 tbsp smoked paprika

3 tbsp mild chilli powder

3 tbsp balsamic vinegar

3 tbsp olive oil

500g belly pork, cubed (outdoor bred if you can source well)

This is where being able to eat fat and lose weight is at its tastiest. Belly pork is great value and takes on flavour well. This works well on the barbeque too.

Method

1. Preheat the oven to 190°c / 375°f.
2. In a bowl, combine the spices with the vinegar and oil, then add the pork and stir until you have an even coating.
3. Place onto an oven tray and bake for 35 minutes.

Cook's Note

- You can place these on cocktail sticks if you are serving tapas.
- If you leave out the vinegar, this can be fine for Phase 1 too.

Hot and Spicy Prawns

- Serves 2
- Phase 1

Ingredients

2 tbsp olive oil

2 chillies, deseeded and chopped

2 cloves of garlic, finely sliced

16 large prawns

1 lemon, halved

Method

1. Heat the olive oil in a frying pan.
2. When the oil is hot, add the chillies and garlic and fry for 1 minute.
3. Add the prawns and fry for a further 4-5 minutes, turning regularly.
4. Transfer the prawns to a warmed dish and pour the oil from the frying pan over the prawns.
5. Squeeze the lemon juice over the prawns, making sure no pips fall in.
6. Serve immediately.

Beef and Horseradish with Tomato

- Serves 4
- Phase 2

Ingredients

6 tbsp horseradish

6 slices of cold beef

18 cherry tomatoes, halved

Cocktail sticks

A simple but tasty meaty tapas dish.

Method

1. Take a tablespoon of horseradish and spread it over the beef slice, then roll it up.
2. Cut the beef into 1cm pieces and thread onto a cocktail stick.
3. Top and tail the cocktail stick with a cherry tomato.

Cook's Note

- You can get Horseradish sauces without sugar and other nasties. Horseradish (of course), vinegar, oil and seasoning are likely ingredients. Mustard and egg yolk are also possible. You don't need sugar or flour or anything you don't recognise. You can always make your own with 100g of peeled and minced horseradish root, 50ml white wine vinegar and salt and pepper to taste.
- Keep in the fridge until ready to serve.

Chorizo, Halloumi and Blueberry Kebabs

- Serves 4
- Phase 3

Ingredients

200g dried chorizo sausage, sliced

100g halloumi, sliced

100g blueberries

4 kebab sticks

Halloumi is a cooking cheese: once it has been under the grill or barbeque you get a crispy outside and a chewy cheesy middle. It's quite salty, so the blueberries help to balance this out and the chorizo gives a kick of spice.

Method

1. Preheat the oven to 200°c / 400°f.
2. Thread the chorizo onto the kebab sticks alternately with halloumi and blueberries.
3. Grill each side of the kebab for 4 minutes.

Cook's Note

- Serve with a green salad, or eat them straight off the stick.

Soups

When people hear that I follow a gluten-free diet they ask: "what do you eat instead of sandwiches for lunch?" – and the answer is often soup or salad.

I always like to make soup with the option of turning it into a sauce, so that I have a supply of freshly made sauces in the freezer. For example, the tomato soup recipe can be used as a Bolognese sauce, or add chilli and use for a chilli beef pie recipe.

The butternut squash soup can be used as a curry sauce by adding chicken and a bag of spinach.

If you like spicy food, then turn your favourite curry sauce into a soup.

Soup is really filling, and if it's blended it's easy to digest. Granny wasn't mad when she said "chicken soup will make you better"!

Spiced Butternut Squash and Coconut (can be V)

- Serves 4
- Phase 3

Ingredients

800g butternut squash, peeled, deseeded and cubed

4 tbsp olive oil

3 chillies, whole

1 tsp garam masala

1 tsp ground cumin

6 garlic cloves

1 onion, peeled and finely chopped

600ml chicken or vegetable stock

200ml coconut milk

1 lime

Salt and black pepper for seasoning

Coconut milk makes this soup so rich and creamy without the need for dairy products. This can be used as a curry sauce too. Just add meat or fish of your choice with extra vegetables.

Method

1. Preheat the oven to 200°c / 400°f.
2. Drizzle the butternut squash with half the olive oil. Toss with the chillies and spices.
3. Roast for 20 minutes. Scatter over the garlic and roast for a further 30 minutes.
4. Heat the remaining olive oil in a pan. Add the onion to the pan and allow to soften.
5. When the butternut squash is tender, discard 2 of the chillies.
6. Put the spiced butternut squash into a blender or food processor, with the remaining chilli, onion and 200ml stock. Blend everything until smooth.
7. Return the liquid mixture to the pan and add the coconut milk and the remaining stock.
8. Simmer for 20 minutes. Halve the lime and squeeze in the juice, making sure that no lime pips fall into the pan. Season well and serve hot.

Cook's Note

- Vegetable stock adds another valuable vegetarian recipe to your repertoire. Chick peas could be added to make a main meal curry, or just enjoy the soup.
- We've marked this as Phase 3 for The Harcombe Diet because it is strictly a mix meal. Per portion, 200g of butternut squash contains approximately 24g of carbohydrate and no fat; 50ml of coconut milk contains approximately 12g of fat and 3g of carbohydrate. However, this could be used as the base for a Phase 2 fat or carb meal – especially if something is added to make the sauce go further (and therefore each portion of sauce becomes smaller). Chicken would go really well, for example. Plus – when you are doing well in Phase 2, a little flex like this is really not going to spoil progress. Sticking to real food is the single best thing that you can do.

Mean Green Soup – Spinach, Celeriac and Courgette (V)

- Serves 4
- Phase 1

Ingredients

2 tbsp of olive oil

1 onion, peeled and finely chopped

1 celeriac, peeled and cubed

3 small courgettes, peeled and chopped into small pieces

600ml boiling water

2 tbsp vegetable bouillon

1 (100g) bag of spinach

Celeriac makes a great alternative to potatoes without the high carb intake and it gives this soup a lovely thick texture.

Method

1. Heat the oil in a large pan.
2. Fry the onion in the olive oil for a few minutes, until it starts to soften.
3. Add the celeriac and courgettes to the pan.
4. Add the water and bouillon powder to the pan then leave to simmer for 20 minutes, or until the vegetables are soft.
5. Add the bag of spinach and place the lid on the pan. The spinach will wilt in a few minutes.
6. Remove from the heat and blend everything in a blender or food processor.
7. Reheat gently to serve.

Cook's Note

- Add a swirl of double cream for a Phase 2, creamier soup.

Beetroot Soup (can be V)

- Serves 4
- Phase 1

Ingredients

2 tbsp olive oil

1 onion, peeled and finely chopped

3 large fresh beetroot, peeled and cubed

10 cherry tomatoes, halved

2 beef (or vegetable) stock cubes

350ml of water

2 garlic cloves

Beetroot has a natural sweet, earthy taste and is full of fibre. Beware of having purple palms after chopping up the beetroot!

Method

1. Heat the olive oil in a large saucepan.
2. Add the onion to the pan and cook for a few minutes, until it looks translucent.
3. Add the beetroot to the pan and leave it to sweat for 5 minutes on a low heat. Then add the cherry tomatoes.
4. Add the stock cubes, water, and garlic and bring to the boil. Leave to simmer for 30 minutes.
5. Liquidise using a stick blender then reheat gently to serve hot.

Cook's Note

- Beef stock complements the beetroot flavour really well, but this is another recipe where vegetable stock can be used instead for a vegetarian recipe.

Spiced Parsnip and Apple (can be V)

- Serves 4
- Phase 2

Ingredients

20g butter

1 tbsp olive oil

2 onions, peeled and diced

2 garlic cloves, chopped

3 tbsp curry powder

700g parsnips, peeled and diced

2 pints vegetable/ chicken stock

Pinch of salt

Pinch of pepper

175g cooking apples, peeled, cored and diced

If you have parsnips left over (maybe after Thanks giving or Christmas? Or just in the seasonal organic delivery veg box), then this is a great way to use them up.

Method

1. Heat the butter and olive oil in a large sauce pan, until the butter starts to foam.
2. Add the onions and soften for about 5 minutes before adding the garlic. Leave to cook for a further 2 minutes.
3. Mix together with the curry powder and stir.
4. Add the parsnips to the pan along with the apples.
5. Stir well and pour in the stock, and add some seasoning.
6. Leave to simmer gently for half an hour without a lid.
7. Remove from the heat and blend everything in a blender or food processor.
8. Place back onto the heat and warm through. Serve hot.

Cook's note

- Opt for vegetable stock for another great vegetarian option.

Roast Pepper and Sun-dried Tomato (V)

- Serves 4
- Phase 1

Ingredients

500g salad tomatoes

4 garlic cloves

1 onion, halved

3 red peppers, halved and deseeded

2 tbsp olive oil

25g butter

2 celery sticks, finely chopped

450ml vegetable stock

2 tbsp tomato purée

1 tbsp sun-dried tomato paste

1 tsp chilli flakes

Pinch of salt

Pinch of pepper

I always save a portion of this soup for my freezer so I have a quick Bolognese sauce at the ready.

Method

1. Preheat the oven to 200°c / 400°f.
2. Place the tomatoes, garlic, onion and pepper halves (cut side down) onto a baking tray and drizzle with olive oil.
3. Bake on the top shelf of the oven for 30 minutes, until roasted.
4. Melt the butter over a medium heat and sauté the celery for 4-5 minutes.
5. Add the vegetable stock, tomato purée, sun-dried tomato paste and chilli flakes together and mix well.
6. Remove from the heat and leave to one side.
7. When the vegetables are roasted, remove the peel from the garlic and onion, and roughly chop them. Add to the pan along with the tomatoes.
8. Place back on a low to medium heat for 20 minutes.
9. Blend with a hand blender, until smooth.
10. Season well and gently simmer, until the soup is at a suitable temperature to eat.

Mains

I often get a text message from my husband, "What's for tea?" So now I say, "Look at the planner!"

To make things simple, every few months I like to make a planner for our meals. '7 dinners for 7 days'. We vote as a family for our favourites and make sure there is always a mix of chicken, red meat (because it's far more nutritious than white meat), some fish and a creamy dish. Then I make a shopping list and we have these dishes for a while until we fancy a change. It's much easier to live like this instead of getting home, opening the fridge and wondering what's for tea. You also save money, as you only buy what you need.

Of course, if you have guests or fancy something different on the weekend, then you can – It's your tummy! So fill it full of lovely (real) food.

Oven Roasted Ratatouille (V)

- Serves 4
- Phase 1

Ingredients

2 large onions, peeled and diced

2 aubergines, diced

2 peppers, deseeded and diced (red or yellow)

2 courgettes, sliced

6 cloves garlic, peeled and chopped

1 tbsp olive oil

1 tbsp smoked paprika

Pinch of salt

1/2 tbsp mixed herbs

1kg passata

Ratatouille is a great staple meal. The recipe uses lower starchy vegetables and passata so it can be used with either carb, or fat meals. Passata is a thick tomato sauce made from sieved tomatoes. It comes without the added sugar and nasties of commercial sauces and is readily available in super markets. I like to make this in bulk and freeze it in portions.

Method

1. Preheat the oven to 175°C/ 350°F.
2. Place the vegetables onto a large baking tray or two smaller ones (you want one layer).
3. Drizzle over some olive oil and sprinkle over the spices, salt and herbs.
4. Roast for 15 minutes and stir through. Roast for a further 20 minutes.
5. Once cooked, remove the tray and pour over the passata.
6. Stir through and serve.

Cook's Note

- Feel free to spice this up with chilli powder, or any other flavour you'd like to add.
- For a fat meal, try using it as a sauce with meat balls and cheese, or as a side for a salmon fillet or chicken.
- For a carb meal serve with brown rice, quinoa, jacket potato or sweet potato wedges.

Pea, Mint and Feta Frittata (V)

- Serves 4
- Phase 2

Ingredients

2 tbsp olive oil

1 large onion, peeled and finely diced

200ml boiled water

200g frozen peas

1 courgette, peeled and grated

6 eggs

100ml double cream

8 fresh mint leaves, finely chopped

100g feta cheese, cubed

100g cheddar, grated

Frittata or crustless quiche can work with so many fillings, but this one is a little bit special and it is great for vegetarians.

Method

1. Preheat the grill to 175°C / 350°F.
2. Heat the olive oil in a pan.
3. Add the onion to the pan and leave to sauté on a low heat.
4. Pour the boiled water over the peas in a large bowl and leave to one side to defrost.
5. Add the courgette to the onion and stir well.
6. Drain the peas and add these to the pan.
7. Put the eggs and cream in a mixing bowl, and whisk until you have a thick, pale yellow mixture. Then stir in the mint.
8. Pour the egg mixture into the frying pan and turn up the heat to help seal the egg. Then mix both mixtures together.
9. Spread the feta and cheddar over the frittata.
10. Turn down the heat to the lowest setting and cook for 5 minutes.
11. Place under the grill to brown off for a further 3 minutes.

Cook's Note

- Serve warm or cold, for breakfast, lunch or tea.

Slow Cooker Beef and Aubergine Curry

- Serves 6
- Phase 1

Ingredients

2 tbsp olive oil

750g braising beef, diced

1 onion, peeled and finely diced

2 large garlic cloves, finely diced

4 tbsp of garam masala

2 tbsp smoked paprika

1 tbsp chilli powder

800g tomatoes, chopped (two 400g tins will work well)

100g tomato purée

150ml water

4 large aubergines, diced

Salt and pepper

(100g grated cream of coconut)

Handful of coriander, finely chopped

As a nutritionist, knowing the nutritional content of red meat, it always amazes me that it gets such a bad press. Red meat is far more nutritious than white meat – and tastier. It is full of B vitamins – our mind, mood and muscle vitamins – and of course rich in iron and zinc. Ideally try to source beef from pasture living cattle – this is important for your health, the animal's health and the health of the planet (cows rejuvenate soil in a natural circle of life with the grass and micro flora that they swallow, host and regurgitate).

Method

1. Preheat the oven to 175°C / 350°F.
2. Heat the oil in a large non-stick pan and add the beef. Keep stirring to seal each side.
3. Add the onion and garlic to the pan. Turn the heat down to the lowest setting.
4. Add the spices to the beef and pour over the tomatoes, tomato puree and water. Leave to simmer.
5. Place the aubergine onto two baking trays and sprinkle with olive oil. Season with salt and pepper.
6. Place in the oven for 30 minutes.
7. When the aubergine is cooked, add it to the curry and stir through.
8. Simmer on low for 3 hours.
9. When you are ready to serve, add the grated creamed coconut and coriander.

Cook's Note

- Serve warm or cold, for breakfast, lunch or tea.
- Serve hot with our non bread (see side dishes for the recipe)
- Strict Phase 1 would leave out the coconut cream, but each portion ends up with approximately 15g so you may choose not to worry about this for the benefit of the richness of the flavour. The famous Harcombe Diet butternut squash curry uses coconut cream with the same caveat – probably worth the flex for the flavour benefit, but leave out if you're an all or nothing type.

Beef Bourguignon

- Serves 6
- Phase 2

Ingredients

2 tbsp olive oil

200g bacon

1kg braising beef, diced

3 shallots, peeled and finely diced

2 tbsp corn flour

1 large carrot, finely chopped

1 stick celery, finely chopped

200g button mushrooms, halved

500ml red wine (I use a Merlot)

200ml water

3 beef stock cubes

Handful of thyme, chopped

This recipe includes a decent dose of red wine, which goes really well with the beef in terms of flavour and it's not a bad 'digestif' too! I always serve this on Boxing Day, because it's great to make ahead for a crowd and to leave to simmer. A rich classic, which I like to serve with mashed celeriac and green vegetables.

Method

1. Heat the oil in a large non-stick pan.
2. Fry the bacon until brown and crispy.
3. Put the beef in the pan and then fry it until it is sealed on all sides.
4. Stir the shallots into the pan and sprinkle the corn flour into the pan – coating the pieces of beef.
5. Add the carrot, celery and mushrooms to the pan.
6. Pour in the wine and water, and cook on a low heat for 3 hours.
7. When you are ready to serve, crumble in the stock cubes and thyme, then turn up the heat to thicken the sauce.
8. Serve hot.

Cook's Note

- Don't worry about the tiny amount of corn flour. There will be so little in each portion as not to worry about and it is important for thickening. Don't worry unduly about the red wine either – much of it burns off in cooking.

Luxurious Low Carb Fish Pie

- Serves 6
- Phase 2

Ingredients

500g (1 large) celeriac, peeled and cubed

500ml boiling water

Salt and pepper

50g butter

25g corn flour

250ml whole milk

100g strong cheddar, grated

2 salmon fillets, diced

250g cod steaks (or other white fish), diced

250g smoked haddock, diced

200g prawns

100g frozen peas

1 tsp fresh or dried parsley

Oily fish, such as salmon, is rich in essential omega-3 oils. Essential in nutrition means something that we must consume in our diet, because the body can't make it. The essential fats (omega-3 and omega-6) are called essential for this reason: we can't make them, so we must eat them. This low carb fish pie has been a true family favourite in our house, since my daughter was a baby. It is a great way to introduce fish to children and even grownups who aren't fish fans. They will be after this.

Method

1. Preheat the oven to 175°C / 350°F.
2. Put the celeriac in a large saucepan.
3. Pour boiling water over the celeriac and add 1/2 a teaspoon of salt. Bring everything to the boil and leave to simmer for 15 minutes until the celeriac is soft.
4. While the celeriac cooks, make your roux sauce by melting the butter in a large non-stick pan.
5. Using a wooden spoon, stir in the corn flour until it combines to make a smooth paste. Season with salt and pepper.
6. Pour in the milk and stir through until you have a thick white sauce. Add 50g of the grated cheese to the mix.
7. Add the fish to the white sauce with the peas and leave to cook through for 10 minutes. Then transfer to a Pyrex dish.
8. The celeriac should be ready for mashing. Work quickly to mash it, then cover the fish evenly. Sprinkle with the remaining cheese.
9. Place on the middle shelf in the oven and bake for 30 minutes. Serve hot with the (fresh) parsley sprinkled on top.

Cook's Note

- Don't worry about the tiny amount of corn flour. There will be so little in each portion as not to worry about and it is important for thickening.
- We didn't suggest an alternative milk for this one, as the cheese makes it unsuitable for those who can't tolerate dairy – sorry!

Slow Roast Chinese Duck with Egg Pancake Rolls

- Serves 4
- Phase 2

Ingredients

4 duck breasts

4 tsp salt

3 tbsp gluten-free soy sauce (tamari)

3tbsp balsamic vinegar

3 tbsp of water

1 tbsp five spice

3 cloves of garlic, chopped

1 inch piece of ginger, peeled and grated

200g blackberries

For the pancakes

1 tbsp olive oil

3 eggs

Pinch of baking power

1 carrot, grated

Bunch of fresh coriander, chopped

Duck is a quite a fatty meat, so this is a hearty fat meal with The Harcombe Diet. This dish sends a lovely aroma around the house while cooking and if you are missing Chinese food then it's certainly worth the effort.

Method

For the Duck

1. Preheat the oven to 150°C / 300°F.
2. Heat a heavy based frying pan without any oil, until smoking hot.
3. Score the skin of the duck breasts and rub with a tsp of salt.
4. Place the duck breasts skin side down and fry for 5 minutes.
5. Place the duck breasts in an oven dish.
6. In a bowl, mix together the soy sauce, balsamic vinegar and water. Add the five spice, garlic and ginger, then pour over the duck.
7. Place the blackberries around the duck breasts.
8. Place on a middle shelf in the oven for 3 hours.
9. Remove from the oven and leave to cool for 15 minutes.
10. Shred the duck and sieve through any remaining sauce and leave to one side.

For the pancakes

1. Heat the oil in a small frying pan.
2. Whisk the eggs with the baking powder.
3. For 4 pancakes pour in one quarter of the mixture and fry like a pancake.
4. Repeat the process until you have 4 pancakes.
5. Fill the pancake with duck, carrot and coriander salad and drizzle any remaining juices from the pan. Then roll up to serve.

St. David's Day Cawl

- Serves 6
- Phase 2 (can be adapted to Phase 1)

Ingredients

2 tbsp olive oil

600g lamb, boned shoulder, diced

2 onions, peeled and roughly chopped

2 celery sticks, sliced

2 carrots, peeled and sliced

600ml lamb or vegetable stock

2 parsnips, peeled and chopped

1 small swede, peeled and chopped

2 leeks, trimmed and sliced

1 large celeriac, peeled and chopped

250ml red wine

Dash of Worcester sauce

2 tsp dried thyme

Salt and pepper to taste

I'm proud to be Welsh and it's traditional to serve this recipe on St David's day but it can be eaten at anytime of the year.
Soups and stews have been shown to keep people fuller for longer due to the water content. Get yourself a soup flask and take some to work for lunch – beats sandwiches any day!

Method

1. Heat the oil in a large pan.
2. Stir the lamb in with the oil for a few minutes until the meat is brown.
3. Add the onions, celery and carrots and then turn the heat down to the lowest setting and place the lid on the pan to let the vegetables sweat through.
4. Pour in the stock and leave to simmer on low for 2 hours.
5. Add the parsnips, swede, leeks and celeriac to the pan.
6. Pour in the wine, Worcester sauce, and thyme and leave to cook on a medium heat for a further 35 minutes until the vegetables are softened.
7. Season well and serve.

Cook's Note

- If there is any liquid left over you can keep it as a stock for gravy.
- You can leave out the red wine and Worcester sauce to make this a Phase 1 dish. The dash of Worcester sauce will be fine to leave in – even in Phase 1 – to be honest.

Slow Cooked Beef Ragu

- Serves 8
- Phase 2 (can be adapted to Phase 1)

Ingredients

2 tbsp olive oil

250g smoked pancetta/bacon, finely diced

1kg braising beef, diced

1 large onion, peeled and finely chopped

2 cloves garlic, peeled and chopped

2 sticks celery, finely chopped

8 salad tomatoes, quartered

2 carrots, peeled and grated

2 x 500g cartons of passatta

6 tbsp tomato puree

1 glass dry white wine

1 tsp dried Italian herbs

2 tsp corn flour (optional)

This is a traditional Bolognese sauce with a twist, using chunky pieces of beef and pancetta/bacon, which is slow cooked for several hours in a rich tomato and herb sauce.
This dish is a perfect 'bulk cooking' recipe. When making a slow cooked dish I tend to make it in bulk and freeze anything left over.

Method

1. Heat the olive oil in a large pan, then add the pancetta/bacon and cook on a high heat for 5 minutes. This helps to get a really nice base flavour for the ragu.

2. Add the beef and cook for 5 minutes, stirring continuously to make sure each piece is sealed.

3. Add the onion, garlic, celery, quartered tomatoes and carrots and sauté with the meat for 5 minutes.

4. Add the passatta, tomato puree and wine along with the herbs.

5. Bring everything to the boil and then turn the heat down to the lowest setting and leave the dish to simmer for 3 hours without a lid. The sauce will thicken during the cooking process. If you would like a thicker sauce, add a couple of teaspoons of corn flour to a cup half filled with cold water to make a paste. Use a fork to mix through any lumps and then stir this into your sauce.

Cook's Note

- I like to serve this with salad and garlic dough balls.
- The best part about getting to know your local butcher is that s/he will prepare meat for you. I always ask mine to dice up my meat, which saves so much time in the kitchen.

Breton Chicken

- Serves 4
- Phase 2

Ingredients

2 tbsp olive oil

1 large onion, peeled and diced

4 garlic cloves, chopped

4 chicken breasts, cubed

1 gammon steak, cubed (or bacon)

2 tbsp corn flour or arrowroot powder

300ml double cream

200g cheddar cheese, grated

300ml water

1 large broccoli, chopped into small florets

1 large leek, sliced

Here is why I don't often eat carbs – because I can eat things like this without gaining weight. Smoked bacon with chicken in a creamy sauce – what's not to like?

Method

1. Heat the oil in a large non-stick pan.
2. Add the onion and garlic to the pan and sauté for 5 minutes, on a low heat.
3. Add the chicken breasts and gammon. Stir until all of the meat is sealed.
4. Sprinkle over the corn flour, making sure that you coat all of the meat.
5. Pour in the cream, grated cheese and water.
6. Add the broccoli and leeks to the pan and leave to simmer on the lowest heat for 30 minutes – until the sauce thickens.
7. Serve hot.

Cook's Note

• Don't worry about the tiny amount of corn flour. There will be so little in each portion as not to worry about and it is important for thickening.

Courgette Carbonara (V)

- Serves 2-4
- Phase 2

Ingredients

20g butter

300g smoked bacon

1 shallot or small onion, peeled and chopped

2 cloves garlic, chopped

2 medium courgettes, spiralised

150ml double cream

2 egg yolks

100g Parmesan cheese, grated

Handful of fresh parsley, chopped

Courgette pasta has become really popular in recent years. It makes a great alternative to pasta as it cooks quickly and takes on flavour really well, plus its loaded with fibre and vitamin C.
This sauce is so luxurious with cream, egg and smoked bacon, and it's so quick to make.
I'm so glad I don't count calories because If I did, this recipe would be off the scale! As you will be learning from Zoë, calories are not equal so with that in mind eat away!

Method

1. Heat the butter in a pan and fry the bacon until crispy.

2. Add the onion and garlic to the pan and cook for 5 minutes on low heat. Then add the courgette.

3. In a bowl, whisk the cream with the egg yolks and pour into the pan. Turn the heat up and stir through until the cream thickens.

4. Sprinkle the Parmesan over the top and add parsley if you wish.

Cook's Note

- The Harcombe Diet recommends avoiding smoked bacon (and other smoked foods) if you suffer from Candida. Hopefully you're fine with some in Phase 2, as the smoked bacon really makes this dish.
- Serve with a rocket and tomato salad.

Sweet Potato and Vegetable Curry (V)

- Serves 4
- Phase 2

Ingredients

600g sweet potatoes, peeled and cubed

1 tbsp olive oil

1 onion, peeled and chopped

1 red pepper, deseeded and chopped

4 tbsp of garam masala

1 tsp chilli powder

1 courgette, peeled and chopped

800g chopped tomatoes (2x400g tins will be fine)

400g tin chickpeas, drained

Salt and pepper to taste

This is a lovely vegetarian dish, full of spice. By roasting the sweet potatoes, it helps to hold them together when you add them to the curry.

Method

1. Preheat the oven to 1705C / 350°F.
2. Drizzle the sweet potatoes with olive oil and a pinch of salt.
3. Roast for 25 minutes or until golden brown/soft.
4. Fry the onion, add the pepper, garam masala, chilli powder, courgette and cook for approximately 5-7 minutes.
5. Add the chopped tomatoes and chickpeas and leave to simmer while the sweet potato cooks.
6. Remove the sweet potatoes from the oven and add them to the pan. Stir them gently into the tomato sauce, so that they don't break up.
7. Season well.

Wrapped Pork Mince

- Serves 4
- Phase 1

Ingredients

1 green cabbage

150ml boiling water

1 tbsp olive oil

1 red onion, peeled and finely chopped

2 spring onions, finely chopped

2 garlic cloves, finely chopped

1 tsp chilli flakes/powder

1 tsp ground cumin

1 tsp garam masala

500g pork mince

150g passata

Salt and pepper

This recipe uses cabbage leaves. Green leafy vegetables are the king in terms of plant nutrition and fibre, so it's worth adding them to your daily diet. Cabbage can also be finely chopped and added to salad.

Method

1. Preheat the oven to 175°C / 350°F.
2. Remove the cabbage base and peel off 8 full leaves.
3. Fill a saucepan with boiling water and add the cabbage leaves, leave to simmer for 5 minutes.
4. Fry the olive oil in a separate pan. When the oil is heated, add the onions, garlic, chilli, cumin and garam masala and cook for 5 minutes, stirring.
5. Add the mince and cook until browned.
6. Mix in the passata and add salt and pepper to taste.
7. Spoon 2-3 tbsp of mince mix into the centre of a cabbage leaf and roll up to make a parcel. Place join down into an oven proof dish.
8. Repeat with the remaining cabbage leaves and then bake for 15 minutes.

Cook's Note

- If you have any mince meat mixture left you can add a tin of chopped tomatoes and serve as a chilli dish.

Curried Kebabs

- Makes 10 kebabs
- Phase 2
(Can be adapted to phase 1)

I'm always thrilled when someone suggests a BBQ, as there are so many real food treats to be had. These kebabs are perfect to take along as your contribution to a BBQ. Plus, it doesn't have to be summer to enjoy these, you can cook them under the grill all year round.

Ingredients

450g meat, diced (pork, chicken, beef or a mixture)

4 tbsp olive oil

½ tsp cumin powder

½ tsp cardamom powder

¼ tsp garam masala

¼ tsp chilli powder

2 cloves garlic, crushed

1 lemon, halved

1 red and 1 yellow pepper, deseeded and chopped

20-30 button mushrooms (optional)

Barbecue skewers

Method

1. Cut the meat into 2-3cm cubes.
2. Mix the oil, spices and garlic. Squeeze in the lemon juice, ensuring no lemon pips fall into the mixture.
3. Cover the meat with the mixture and marinate for 60-90 minutes.
4. Alternate the pepper with the meat cubes and whole mushrooms as you slide them onto the skewers.
5. Barbecue, or grill under a high flame, for 10 minutes.

Cook's Note

- Serve with grilled or barbecued aubergine slices or any other barbecued/ grilled vegetables (courgettes work really well too).
- Leave out the mushrooms for a Phase 1 option.

Baked Meaty Meatballs

- Makes 20 meatballs
- Phase 2

Ingredients

500g beef mince

100g liver of your choice (I use chicken)

200g pancetta

1 onion, peeled and chopped

3 cloves garlic, chopped

Handful of fresh basil, finely chopped

2 eggs

2 tbsp olive oil

250ml red wine

1kg passata

1 red pepper, finely chopped

200g Parmesan cheese, grated

I've heard Zoë saying at conferences that she has struggled to find a more nutritious food than liver (even though she doesn't like it!) I think she might like this. Liver is a phenomenal source of vitamin A, B vitamins and a terrific all rounder for minerals from copper to zinc. It's really good to include liver in the family diet, therefore, so that even children get to like this genuine super food from an early age. I sneak liver in to recipes such as Bolognese and stews and my daughter loves them.

Method

1. Preheat the oven to 175°C / 350°F.
2. Add the raw minced beef, liver and pancetta into the food processor with the onion, garlic, basil and egg and blend everything together.
3. Heat the olive oil in a frying pan.
4. Shape the mixture into meatballs and fry these to seal. Once sealed place in an oven dish.
5. Pour over the red wine, passata, and red pepper. Top with Parmesan and bake for 45 minutes.

Spanish Stew

- Serves 4
- Phase 1

Ingredients

2 tbsp olive oil

1 large onion, peeled and chopped

4 chorizo cooking sausages, sliced

4 chicken breasts, diced

1 courgette, chopped

1 red pepper, deseeded and chopped

1 yellow pepper, deseeded and chopped

3 cloves garlic, chopped

100g of spinach

3 x 400g tins of chopped tomatoes

4 tbsp tomato purée

3 tbsp smoked paprika

2 tbsp chilli powder

2 handfuls of green olives

I love one-pot dishes. This one is quick to put together and would work in a slow cooker too. It's full of Mediterranean flavours, which give a rich tomato sensation. I often bulk cook this recipe and keep portions in the freezer.

Method

1. Heat the olive oil in a frying pan. Once the oil is hot, add the onion.
2. Add the chorizo sausages and cook them for a couple of minutes to release the spices.
3. Add the chicken breasts and cook for 5 minutes.
4. Once the chicken has browned, add the courgette, peppers, garlic and spinach to the pan.
5. Stir in the chopped tomatoes and tomato purée.
6. Add the chilli powder and paprika, followed by the olives.
7. Leave to simmer without a lid for 30 minutes.

Stuffed Chilli Peppers

- Serves 4
- Phase 2

Ingredients

200g left over Bolognese (SEE PAGE 87) or chilli beef mixture (SEE PAGE 117)

2 yellow peppers, halved and deseeded

100g cheddar cheese, grated

This recipe is helpful for when you have some left over chilli or Bolognese and wonder what to do with it.

Method

1. Preheat the oven to 175°C / 350°F.
2. Spoon the left over mixture into the peppers evenly.
3. Sprinkle the peppers with the cheese.
4. Place the peppers on an oven tray and bake for 30 minutes.

Tuna Steaks and Salsa

- Serves 2
- Phase 1

Ingredients

2 limes, juiced

1 garlic clove, chopped

2 tuna steaks

1 red pepper, deseeded and chopped

2 spring onions, chopped

Handful of fresh coriander, chopped

3 tomatoes, chopped

1 fresh chilli, deseeded and chopped

1 tbsp olive oil

1/2 a lime

Fresh tuna steaks are much tastier than the variety found in tins. If you have a fishmonger near you then go and see what they have in stock. This recipe works well with swordfish too.

Method

1. Marinade the tuna steaks overnight in the juice of 1 lime and garlic.

2. Grill for 5 minutes each side.

3. To make the salsa, mix together the pepper, spring onions, coriander, tomatoes and chilli. Then squeeze in the juice of a lime and a tablespoon of olive oil.

4. Spoon the salsa onto a plate and place the tuna on top with a wedge of lime.

Meat Feast Pizza

- Serves 2
- Phase 2

Ingredients

2 gammon steaks

2 tbsp tomato puree

1 onion, peeled and chopped

100g cheese, grated

2 tsp mixed herbs

This is truly a meat feast, as the whole base is made from gammon. This is a popular family dinner – loved by men (filling) and children (tasty) alike – and it is so simple to make. I serve mine with purple coleslaw (SEE PAGE 122).

Method

1. Grill the gammon steak for about 10 minutes each side.
2. Cover the gammon with tomato puree and add the onion on top.
3. Sprinkle the cheese and herbs over the gammon, on top of the onion.
4. Place the gammon back under the grill until the cheese has toasted.

Hunters Chicken

- Serves 4
- Phase 2

Ingredients

4 chicken breasts

4 rashers smoked bacon

1 x 500g carton of passata

1 tbsp balsamic vinegar

2 heaped tbsp of smoked paprika

3 cloves of garlic, chopped

100g cheddar cheese, grated

So many people ask me for recipes that the whole family will like and this is always a winner. The sauce has a smoky barbeque taste, which is complemented by melted cheese.

Method

1. Preheat the oven to 175°C / 350°F.
2. Wrap the chicken in the bacon and place into a Pyrex dish.
3. Pour the passata into a large mixing bowl. Add the vinegar and stir.
4. Add the paprika, and garlic and combine.
5. Pour the mixture over the chicken and bacon and sprinkle the cheddar over the meat.
6. Bake in the oven for 30 minutes.

Cook's Note

- Serve hot with vegetables or salad.

Stilton and Almond Aubergines (V)

- Serves 2, or 4 as a starter
- Phase 3

Ingredients

2 aubergines

2 tbsp olive oil

100g stilton

50g flaked almonds

Stilton is so strong in taste that you don't need much to get the flavour. Aubergines are sometimes called the steak of the vegetarian world. The two strong flavours and 'meaty' texture of the aubergines, works really well together. Aubergines generally, like peppers, are natural 'containers' in the vegetable world. We are familiar with stuffed peppers, but we can do far more with aubergine 'boats'.

Method

1. Preheat the oven to 175°C / 350°F

2. Cut the aubergine lengthways in half and lay face down on a baking tray. Drizzle with the olive oil and roast for 20 minutes.

3. Remove the baking tray from the oven and turn over the aubergines. Mash the flesh of the aubergine with a fork.

4. Crumble the stilton into the aubergine and top with flaked almonds, then place back in the oven for 10 minutes. Serve hot.

Cook's Note

- Serve on a bed of rocket and sun-dried tomatoes.
- The almonds make this a Phase 3 dish, but it's a tiny mix, so do enjoy this in Phase 2 if you are more of a flexi (as Zoë explains in her books).

Aubergine Pizza

- Serves 4
- Phase 2

Ingredients

2 aubergines

2 tbsp olive oil

4 tbsp tomato purée

100g cheddar cheese, grated

6 rashers of bacon or 250g pancetta, diced

1 onion, peeled and finely sliced

I prefer this over dough based pizza any day! It's so easy to make and lovely with my purple coleslaw (SEE PAGE 122). Lose weight by eating pizza and coleslaw – yes please!

Method

1. Preheat the oven to 175°C / 350°F
2. Cut the aubergine lengthways in half and lay face down on a baking tray. Drizzle with the olive oil and roast for 20 minutes.
3. Remove the baking tray from the oven and turn over the aubergines. Mash the flesh of the aubergine with a fork.
4. Cover the flesh side of the aubergine with tomato puree and top with the cheese, bacon and onion.
5. Place back in the oven for 10 minutes to cook through. Serve hot.

Thai Fish Cakes

- Makes 8 fish cakes
- Phase 1

Ingredients Thai curry paste:

4 tbsp olive oil

One onion, peeled and finely chopped

1 green chilli, deseeded and finely diced

1 inch piece of ginger, peeled and grated

2 cloves garlic, finely chopped

1 stalk of lemon grass, finely chopped

Zest and juice of one lime

1/2 teaspoon salt

Ingredients Fish cakes:

150g skinless salmon

150g prawns

150g skinless cod or other white fish

2 eggs

4 tbsp of Thai curry paste

1 tbsp olive oil

Thai flavours work with fish especially well. The beauty of these fish cakes is that they are not breaded. You can make your own Thai curry paste (with my recipe below) or you can buy one with no sugar/wheat or other unnecessary ingredients.

Method – Thai curry paste

1. Add all of the ingredients into a food processor or blender and pulse until you have a smooth paste.

Cook's Note

• You can freeze the paste in ice cube trays. Once set, pop them out of the tray and store in an airtight container in the freezer. Then the cubes can be defrosted at any time to add to a curry or to use as a marinade for fish or meat.

Method – Fish cakes

1. Add the salmon, prawns and cod to a food processor and blitz.

2. Once blitzed, add the egg and Thai curry paste to the food processor. To bring the mixture together, blitz again.

3. Depending on what size you would like your fishcakes, take a spoonful of the mixture and fry in a small amount of olive oil.

4. Place onto some kitchen towel to absorb any excess oil.

Cook's Note

• To keep warm, place in the oven on a low heat, maybe while you prepare some Thai vegetables to accompany the fish cakes.

Chicken Pasanda

- Serves 4
- Phase 3

Ingredients

600g chicken breasts

4 tbsp Natural Live Yoghurt

2 tsp ground cumin

4 tsp ground coriander

8 cardamom seeds

2 tsp ground turmeric

1 tsp coconut oil

1 onion, peeled and chopped

1 piece ginger, peeled and chopped

1 green chilli pepper, deseeded and chopped

2 garlic cloves, chopped

200ml chicken stock

50g ground almonds

2 tsp garam masala

1 can unsweetened coconut milk

A curry from scratch beats a takeaway any day and, if you have time, this is really worth the effort. Pasanda curries are mild on the curry Richter scale; you can always spice yours up with extra chilli peppers, but the Pasanda base of coconut and almond flavours are wonderful without overpowering.

Method

1. Mix the chicken with the yoghurt and spices and leave to marinate while you prepare the rest of the ingredients.
2. Heat the coconut oil in a pan. Once heated, add the onion and cook for about 10 minutes until the onion has softened.
3. Add the ginger, chilli and garlic. Cook for a further 5 minutes until fragrant.
4. Mix the chicken in with the marinade and continue stirring, until the chicken is coloured.
5. When the chicken is cooked through, then add the stock and cover with a lid. Leave to simmer for 30 minutes.
6. Once simmered, add the ground almonds, coconut milk and garam masala and simmer for a further 5 minutes. Serve hot.

Cook's Note

- Serve with roast cauliflower.

Cottage Pie with Celeriac and Parsnip Mash

- Serves 4
- Phase 2

Ingredients

2 tbsp olive oil

1 onion, peeled and chopped

500g minced beef

2 tbsp of corn flour

1 carrot, grated

1/2 small swede, peeled and grated

2 beef stock cubes

300ml boiling water

3 parsnips, peeled and chopped

1 celeriac, peeled and chopped

100g butter

100g cheddar cheese, grated

Here is a way to have your pie and eat it! Think of celeriac as your potato replacement, so for roasties, mash, soups and more, it's the perfect swap.

Method

1. Preheat the oven to 175°C / 350°F.
2. Heat the olive oil in a saucepan. Fry the onion for a couple of minutes; then add the minced beef and fry until brown.
3. Add the corn flour to the beef and stir evenly to coat the meat. Then add the grated carrot and swede.
4. Add the boiling water to a jug and stir in the stock cubes until they melt. Then pour the stock over the mincemeat and stir. The corn flour will help thicken the liquid into a rich gravy.
5. Turn the heat down low and simmer for 30 minutes.
6. While the mixture is simmering, in a separate pan boil the celeriac and parsnips until softened. Once they have softened, add the butter and mash until smooth.
7. Transfer the mixture to a Pyrex dish and cover with the mash and sprinkle with the cheddar. Bake in the oven for 30 minutes.

Cook's Note

- Don't worry about the tiny amount of corn flour. There will be so little in each portion as not to worry about and it is important for thickening.

Salmon Fillet and Pea Purée

- Serves 2
- Phase 1

Ingredients

2 salmon fillets

Salt and black pepper for seasoning

200g frozen peas

50g butter

1/2 lemon, juiced

Green vegetables are highly recommended, but peas are higher in carbohydrate than leafy green vegetables, so peas can feel like quite a treat after days of broccoli and kale! For children, peas have natural sweetness, which should be as much as their sensitive taste buds get to experience. This dish is quick to make and the pea Purée has the most amazing colour.

Method

For the Salmon

1. Preheat the oven to 175°C / 350°F.
2. Place the salmon fillets onto a baking tray and season well.
3. Place on the middle shelf of the oven and bake for 25 minutes.

For the Purée

1. Bring a large pan of salted water to the boil and blanch the peas for 3 minutes.
2. Add the peas to a blender along with a little water, butter and lemon juice.
3. Blitz the peas for no more than 2-3 minutes, until a fairly thick, smooth purée has been achieved.

Cook's Note

- Serve immediately or cool the pea purée as quickly as possible – this will prevent the colour fading.

Garlic Mushroom Chicken

- Serves 4
- Phase 2

Ingredients

2 tbsp of olive oil

1 onion, peeled and finely chopped

6 garlic cloves, finely chopped

2 tbsp corn flour

300ml double cream

Handful of parsley

200g chestnut mushrooms, sliced

4 chicken breasts

150g mozzarella cheese

100g cheddar, grated

This dish is pretty potent and full of garlic – perfect if you've got Candida to attack - plus it tastes great too.

Method

1. Preheat the oven to 175°C/350°F.
2. Heat the oil in a large non-stick pan.
3. Add the onion and garlic to the pan, then turn the heat down low and leave to sauté for 5 minutes.
4. Add the corn flour to the pan and stir through, making sure it coats the onion. Pour in the double cream and fresh parsley.
5. Mix the mushrooms into the sauce and remove the pan from the heat.
6. Place the chicken breasts into a Pyrex dish and pour over the hot sauce.
7. Break up the mozzarella and place it across the top of the chicken, then sprinkle over the cheddar.
8. Place in the middle shelf of the oven and bake for 35 minutes.

Cook's Note

- Serve hot with salad or vegetables.
- Don't worry about the tiny amount of corn flour. There will be so little in each portion as not to worry about and it is important for thickening.

Beef Chilli Pie

- Serves 4
- Phase 1 (without the cheese) or Phase 2 (with cheese)

Ingredients

500ml boiling water

1 large celeriac, peeled and cubed

Salt

2 tbsp olive oil

1 onion, peeled and chopped

500g minced beef

1 carrot, grated

2 sticks celery, chopped

1 tbsp dried cumin

1 tbsp garlic powder

1 tbsp chilli powder

1 tbsp smoked paprika

2 x 500g cartons of passata

1/2 tube (75g) tomato purée

3 large handfuls of spinach

100g vintage cheddar cheese, grated

If you like spice, this dish makes a great alternative to cottage pie.

Method

1. Preheat the oven to 175°C / 350°F.
2. Add the celeriac to a pan filled with the boiling water and salt. Boil for 20 minutes until soft.
3. Heat the oil in a large non-stick pan.
4. Add the onion and sauté for a few minutes, then add the beef and cook on a high heat until the meat has browned and started to dry out.
5. Stir in the carrot and celery and add the spices. Then pour in the passata and tomato puree and combine everything together.
6. Place the lid on the pan and simmer for 20 minutes.
7. Add the spinach, which will wilt down quickly and stir through.
8. When the celeriac is ready, mash and season well. Cover the mince mixture with the mash and top with the cheese.
9. Put in the oven and bake for 30 minutes. Serve hot.

Courgette Fritters (V)

- Serves 4
- Phase 3

Ingredients

2 tbsp olive oil

1 onion, peeled and finely chopped

450g courgette, grated

1 tsp salt

2 large eggs

30g Parmesan cheese, grated

30g cheddar cheese, grated

1 tsp mixed herbs

60g ground almonds

1/2 tsp baking powder

Method

1. Heat the olive oil in a frying pan. Once the oil is heated, add the onion and fry it until brown.
2. Season the courgette with the salt, and leave to soak through for 5 minutes. After 5 minutes, tip the mixture onto a clean tea towel and wring out any excess liquid, then add to the onion.
3. Crack the eggs into the pan and stir well.
4. Add the Parmesan, cheddar cheese, mixed herbs, ground almonds, and baking powder to the mixture and then stir thoroughly.
5. Fry until golden and serve.

Cook's Note

- Serve with bacon and poached eggs for a super brunch.
- This is a Phase 3 dish because of the almonds. You can always leave out the almonds to add another Phase 2 dish to your menu options.

Sides

Side dishes can transform plain meat and fish dishes into a completely new eating adventure. Here you'll find a tasty selection that will liven up your dinner.

Purple Coleslaw (V)

- Serves 4-6
- Phase 2

Ingredients

1 small purple cabbage, finely sliced

1/2 red onion, peeled and finely sliced

2 large carrots, grated

6 tablespoons speedy mayo – (SEE PAGE 124)

Method

1. In a large mixing bowl add the sliced cabbage, diced onion and grated carrot and mix thoroughly.
2. Pour over the speedy mayonnaise and combine.
3. Store the mayo in an airtight container until ready to serve.

Moroccan Tagine (V)

- Serves 6
- Phase 2 or 1 (with slight adjustment)

Ingredients

2 large butternut squash, peeled, deseeded and cubed

4 tbsp olive oil

Pinch of salt

2 red peppers, deseeded and chopped

2 aubergines, cubed

1 large red onion, peeled and diced

6 garlic cloves

1 inch piece of ginger, peeled and grated

2 x400g tinned tomatoes

2 x 500g cartons of passata

2 tbsp cumin

1/2 tsp cinnamon

Handful of fresh coriander, finely chopped

4 fresh apricots, chopped (optional)

This is a great staple side dish, which works equally well with meat, fish or pulses. You can use it as a slow cooker sauce for Moroccan beef or lamb Tagine, by adding diced chunks of either meat.

Method

1. Preheat the oven to 175°C / 350°F.
2. On one tray, place the butternut squash cubes. Drizzle them with a tablespoon of olive oil and season with salt.
3. On a second tray, add the peppers and aubergine and drizzle with a tablespoon of olive oil. Also season with salt, and then place both trays into the oven.
4. Heat 2 tablespoons of olive oil in a frying pan.
5. Fry the onion and garlic in the frying pan for a few minutes.
6. Stir the ginger into the mixture.
7. While the vegetables are roasting in the oven, add the chopped tomatoes and passata to the frying pan along with the spices and simmer for 20 minutes.
8. When the roasted vegetables are ready, add them to the frying pan and mix everything thoroughly.
9. Stir in the coriander and fresh apricots.

Cook's Note

- The apricots can be left out for Phase 1, but they will really add to the dish to include them in Phase 2. This can form the base of a fat or carb meal in Phase 2.

Speedy Mayo (V)

- Makes approximately 300-350ml
- Phase 2 (because of the vinegar)

Ingredients

275ml light olive oil

2 free range eggs

2 tbsp of lemon juice

2 tbsp cider vinegar

1 tsp salt

The next time you are in a super market, pick up a jar of low-fat mayonnaise and see how many ingredients you don't recognise. You will also find refined oils. Finally, check the sugar content, compared to a full fat mayo, and you will see there is an interesting difference.
When fat is removed, sugar is often added, by now you should know that fat (in our food) is our friend!
This recipe is certainly speedy and it uses olive oil and eggs as a base so is really natural. You can customise your mayo by adding fresh garlic, herbs, chilli or mustard for yummy alternatives.

Method

1. Add all of the ingredients into the plastic jar.
2. Place the stick blender into the jar and then turn it on.
3. Slowly bring the blender up and then back down until you get a thick pale yellow mayonnaise (It takes approximately 30 seconds).
4. Store in an airtight container at the back of the fridge (It will keep for approximately 5 days).

Cook's Note

- You will need a stick blender and the plastic jar it comes with.

Roast Cauliflower (V)

- Serves 2
- Phase 1

Ingredients

1 head of cauliflower

1 onion, peeled and chopped

Pinch of salt

3 tbsp olive or coconut oil

1 tbsp of spices of choice (I use 1 tbsp of garam masala)

I have had my fair share of cauliflower rice but it doesn't quite do it for me. However, roasting cauliflower does. It's crunchy, oily, salty, and yummy – I'm sure you'll love it too!

Method

1. Preheat oven to 190°C/375°F.
2. Chop up the cauliflower into tiny florets including the stalk (eat that too). Then lay the cauliflower onto a couple of oven trays and sprinkle with oil, salt, and spices.
3. Place into the oven for 25 minutes. Serve warm.

Cook's Note

- If you are using coconut oil, then you will find it is solid at room temperature. To make coconut oil easier to pour you can soften it by putting the amount needed into a cup and placing the cup into a sink with a couple of inches of hot water.
- Fight over any crunchy bits or eat them before anyone sees!

Creamed Spinach (V)

- Serves 2
- Phase 2

Ingredients

2 tbsp olive oil

50g butter, melted

1 onion, peeled and finely diced

100ml double cream

1/2 tsp nutmeg

200g spinach leaves

Pinch of salt

Pinch of pepper

100g Parmesan cheese, grated

This rich creamy dish takes only minutes to make and will transform a piece of chicken, steak or salmon into a luxurious meal.

Spinach has an extremely high nutritional value - It is a good source of vitamins A, B2, C and K, and also contains magnesium, manganese, folate, iron, calcium and potassium.

Method

1. Heat the olive oil and butter in a large non-stick pan.
2. Once the oil is heated, add the onion to the pan and stir thoroughly with a wooden spoon.
3. Turn the heat down to the lowest setting and leave the onion to sauté for a few minutes.
4. Pour in the double cream and nutmeg and then bring to the boil.
5. Add in the spinach and then turn down the heat. Place the lid on the pan and leave for a few minutes until the spinach has wilted.
6. Season with salt and pepper and mix thoroughly with a wooden spoon.
7. Top with Parmesan and serve.

Celeriac Chips (V)

- Serves 4
- Phase 1

Ingredients

1 celeriac, peeled and chopped into chip shapes

Pinch of salt

Water

2 tbsp olive oil

If you are looking for an alternative to potato chips then these are a must. My problem is that I've told so many people about them that when I come to buy a celeriac they have all sold out!

Method

1. Preheat an oven to 200°C / 400°F.
2. Put the celeriac strips into a pan and cover with water. Season with salt and parboil the celeriac for 10 minutes.
3. Transfer the celeriac strips onto a baking tray, drizzle with olive oil and sprinkle with salt. Roast for 20 minutes.

Non Bread (V)

- Makes 2 nons
- Phase 1

Ingredients

2 eggs

1/2 tsp of dried cumin powder

1/2 tsp mustard seeds

1/2 tsp of baking soda

2 tbsp olive oil

This will give you the feel of a 'nann bread' without the wheat. The baking soda is essential to make the non bread rise.

Method

1. In a large mixing bowl, whisk the eggs for 5 minutes until fluffy. Then mix in the cumin, mustard seeds and baking soda.
2. Heat the oil in a large frying pan for a few minutes, as you need to get the oil really hot.
3. Pour in the egg mixture and cook for 3 minutes, then flip over to cook the other side.

Cook's Note

- Serve with salad and curry.

Butternut Bhaji (V)

- Makes 8
- Phase 3

Ingredients

2 tbsp coconut oil
2 onions, peeled and finely sliced
1/2 large butternut squash, peeled, deseeded and grated
1 egg
2 tbsp garam masala
2 heaped tbsp ground almonds
1/2 tsp salt

Traditional bhaji would be gluten-free as they use gram flour (chickpea flour) but many recipes have been adapted and now include wheat flour. This recipe uses grated butternut squash, which gives you a great bhaji texture without the need for any flour. I like to make them when we have a 'curry night'.

Method

1. Preheat oven to 175°C/350°F.

2. Heat the coconut oil in a large non-stick pan
Fry the finely sliced onions and cook on a low heat for 15 minutes until soft and starting to brown

3. Add the grated squash, egg and spices to a mixing bowl. Add the cooked onions, ground almonds and salt and combine. Leave to set for 5 minutes allowing the egg to absorb the almonds

4. Oil a baking tray. Then take a tablespoon of mixture, shape it into your bhaji and place the bhajis onto the tray until the mixture is used up. Season with salt.
Bake for 20 minutes.

Cooks note

- For extra crispy bhajis you can fry them in some hot oil then and then pat them in kitchen roll before serving, to remove any excess oil.
- These freeze well if you batch cook for the week ahead.

Puddings

If you are going to cheat – do it in style!

I do love a 'good pud' and when I'm tempted by pretty little things in bakery windows I quickly remind myself of how awful I would feel if I gave in to the temptation.

If you are going to cheat then make it worth your while, make the effort to buy the best ingredients you can afford and spend time putting together something you really enjoy.

I always advise people to have some cheat recipes up their sleeve for entertaining (as most people won't even think they are 'healthy puds'.)

I recently visited the sweetener section of a supermarket and counted over 20 kinds of sugars and sweeteners! Just because the jar may look healthy it's not always the case. Personally I would use Stevia if something needs sweetening, but the more we can deny a sweet tooth, the quicker it disappears.

Even sweeteners' can cause us to release insulin (the fat storing hormone) and bring our cravings back, so these puddings come with a health warning: If you eat too many too often you may gain weight or awaken your Candida cravings so be careful.

Remember Zoë's advice: don't cheat too much; don't cheat too often; be alert and stay in control!

Gluten-free Pancakes (V)

- Serves 2 / makes 4 small pancakes
- Phase 3

These can be served as a sweet dish with Greek yoghurt and berries or as a savoury dish, with bacon and scrambled egg.

Ingredients

125g ground almonds

1/4 tsp salt

60ml water

2 eggs

1 tsp olive oil

Method

1. Mix the ground almonds and salt with the water.
2. Beat the eggs and stir into the mixture until you have a thick batter.
3. Pour the oil into a frying pan and heat until warm.
4. Add two tablespoons of the mixture for one pancake and fry for one minute each side.

Dark Chocolate Orange and Almond Truffles (V)

- This recipe makes around 40 truffles, so do make them when others are around to share them – or adjust the quantity down accordingly – or freeze any extras quickly!

- Phase 3

Ingredients

1 tin organic coconut milk

50g coconut oil

300g 85% dark chocolate, broken into pieces

1 tbsp orange oil

100g toasted flaked almonds

I started making truffles as gifts for family when I was in my late teens. I now sell them on a large scale to shops and online! There are so many flavours, but I though I would share a few with you here.
Truffles are a great sweet cheat, as they are so rich that you don't need many.
Usually truffles contain cream, but I wanted to create a version that was dairy-free.

Method

1. Pour the coconut milk into a pan and add the coconut oil.
2. Take the pan off the heat and add the dark chocolate and orange oil. Allow the mixture to melt the chocolate and stir well.
3. Cover the mixture and leave to set in the fridge.
4. Toast the flaked almonds on a baking tray for 2 minutes.Then leave to one side.
5. Take a teaspoon of the mixture and shape into a ball to make a truffle. Then roll the truffle in toasted flaked almonds.
6. Store in the freezer or fridge.

Raspberry and Coconut Truffles (V)

- Makes around 40 truffles
- Phase 3

Ingredients

200g 85% dark chocolate, broken into pieces

100g coconut oil

20g freeze-dried raspberries

50ml unsweetened coconut milk

50g desiccated coconut

50g desiccated coconut (for rolling)

Method

1. Place a bowl over a pan of simmering hot water, and pour the chocolate and coconut oil into the bowl. Leave over the heat, stirring occasionally with a wooden spoon, until the mixture has melted.
2. Take the pan off the heat and add the freeze-dried raspberries.
3. Add 50g of the desiccated coconut along with the coconut milk and stir until mixed through.
4. Cover the mixture and leave to set in the fridge.
5. Once set, take a teaspoon of the mixture and shape into a ball to make a truffle.Then roll the truffle in the leftover desiccated coconut.
6. Store in the freezer or fridge.

Egg Yolk Truffles (V)

- Makes 40
- Phase 3

Ingredients

350g 85% dark chocolate, broken into pieces

175g salted butter, cubed

1 tsp vanilla essence

3 egg yolks

Cocoa powder for dusting

Eggs are full of trace minerals, selenium being one of them, which is great for healthy hair, skin and nails. The egg yolk gives such a rich flavour, and without using cream there is more room for more chocolate! You can flavour anyway you wish, but my favourite by far is sea salt and vanilla and then closely followed by chilli. (For the chilli version, just remove the vanilla and add a teaspoon of ground chilli powder).

Method

1. Place a bowl over a pan of simmering hot water, and put the chocolate into the bowl. Leave over the heat, stirring occasionally with a wooden spoon, until the mixture has melted.

2. Once the chocolate has melted, remove the bowl from the pan and add the butter and vanilla essence. Stir until you have a thick chocolate sauce.

3. Using a whisk, whisk in the egg yolks and stir the mixture well. The mixture will become thick.

4. Cover the mixture and leave to set in the fridge.

5. Once set, take a teaspoon of the mixture and shape into a ball to make a truffle.Roll the truffle in the cocoa powder.

6. Store in the fridge or freezer.

Cook's Note

- If you eat them straight from the freezer they last even longer.

Date and Cashew Nut Fudge (V)

- Makes approximately 10 balls
- Phase 3

Ingredients

300g dates

300g cashew nuts

1 tbsp vanilla

This is really high in fruit sugar, but it is a natural alternative to the sticky confectionery option.

Method

1. Blitz the dates, cashew nuts and vanilla in a food processor.
2. Cover the mixture and leave to set in the fridge.
3. Take a teaspoon of the mixture and shape into a ball.
4. Store in the fridge or freezer.

Cook's Note

- These taste their best when frozen.

Apricot and Oat Muesli Bar (V)

- Makes approximately 10 bars
- Phase 3

Ingredients

250g dried apricots

100g raisins

100g desiccated coconut

100g oats

50g butter, melted

If you want to wean anyone off refined sugar, then recipes like this may help in the short term. They are still high in natural sugar though, so keep them for an occasional cheat. These would make great lunch box snacks for children, however – especially on sports day.

Method

1. Place the dried apricots, raisins, desiccated coconut, oats and butter in a food processor. Blitz until combined.
2. Transfer the mixture into a tin or lunch box and pat down until flat.
3. Set in the fridge for a few hours.
4. Once set, slice and keep in airtight container in fridge.

Chocolate Shots (V)

- Makes 8
- Phase 3

Ingredients

300ml double cream

100g 85% dark chocolate, broken into pieces

50g coconut oil (or melted butter)

Flavour of your choice (Brandy, orange, peppermint)

Chocolate desserts can be a good choice when eating out, especially in fancy restaurants, as they usually contain real ingredients such as cream, cocoa powder/very dark chocolate, vanilla and/or eggs. We use a few of these in this recipe, which works well with orange zest or a teaspoon of peppermint oil added.

Method

1. Place the double cream into a non-stick saucepan and leave on a low heat to warm through.
2. Add the chocolate pieces to the cream mixture; then stir through.
3. Add the coconut oil (or butter) and any flavour you wish; then stir thoroughly again.
4. Leave to cool before pouring into ramekins or shot glasses. Then set in the fridge for a few hours or overnight.

Cook's Note

- Will keep well in the fridge for around 4-5 days, or wrap the shots individually in cling film and store standing upright in a Tupperware box in the freezer.

Hazelnut Spread (V)

- Makes a large jar
- Phase 3

Ingredients

200g hazelnuts

4 tbsp honeyor maple syrup

2 tbsp cocoa powder or cacao

4 tbsp boiling water

Pinch of sea salt

Children love chocolate nut spread, but the best known brand, Nutella(R), was 57% sugar last time I checked. That's really not a great way for our most precious people to start their day. This recipe uses honey or maple syrup – still sugars – but in far smaller amounts. I've made this at my children's cookery school sessions and it went down rather well.

Method

1. Preheat the oven to 175°C/350°F.
2. Toast the hazelnuts on a baking tray for 3 minutes.
3. Add the hazelnuts, honey/maple syrup, cocoa powder, boiling water and salt to a food processor and blend for 5 minutes.
4. Leave to set in the fridge.

Cook's Note

- To keep the healthy theme, serve on oat biscuits rather than supermarket bread (which usually has tens of ingredients – many not so nice).

Squidgy Chocolate Brownie (V)

- Makes 16 brownies
- Phase 3

Ingredients

225g 70-85% dark chocolate (the darker you go, the richer the brownies), broken into pieces

225g butter, cubed

2 tsp vanilla extract

3 large eggs (beaten)

150g ground almonds

100g toasted flaked almonds

When I need a cake recipe for an occasion, I use ground almonds as my alternative to flour. Almonds are more nutritious than flour, lower in carbohydrate and thus have a much lower impact on the blood sugar level. Almonds also tick the real food box and are therefore naturally satiating.
A word of caution for those with a sweet tooth – this is a naturally dark chocolate delight – it tastes rich, rather than sweet, but that's a good thing.

Method

1. Preheat the oven to 175°C/350°F.

2. Melt the chocolate and butter gently over a low heat in a heavy-based saucepan.

3. Take the pan off the heat, mix in the vanilla and leave to cool.

4. Beat the eggs into the pan along with the ground almonds and flaked almonds.

5. Turn into a 24cm / 9 inch square baking tin, or use a foil one (which can be peeled away from the brownie square to get the 'cake' out more easily).

6. Bake in the oven for 25-30 minutes, by which time the top will have set, but the mixture will still be gooey. Once cooler, cut carefully, four down, four across, into 16 squidgy squares.

Avocado, Sea Salt and Vanilla Mousse (V)

- Serves 4
- Phase 3

Ingredients

100g 70-85% dark chocolate, broken into pieces.

Pinch sea salt

1 tbsp vanilla essence

50ml almond milk (or cow's milk if you prefer)

2 large ripe avocados, halved and stone removed

This is a wonderful easy recipe, with a dairy-free option. This is so rich that it's best made in shot glasses. If you find it too 'dark' then add a teaspoon of Stevia.

Method

1. Place a bowl over a pan of simmering hot water, and put the chocolate into the bowl. Leave over the heat, stirring occasionally with a wooden spoon, until the mixture has melted.
2. Whisk the melted chocolate until you have a rich sauce.
3. Stir in the salt and vanilla. Remove from the heat and add the almond milk.
4. Scoop out the avocado flesh into a bowl. Using a fork, mash up the avocado and then add to the chocolate mixture.
5. Whisk the mixture until it is thick (you can also use a food processor or blender if you want an even smoother mixture).
6. Transfer into shot glasses or ramekins and leave to cool.

Cook's Note

- You can serve this straight away or keep in the fridge for up to 3 days.

Useful Tables
Measures and Conversions

All of our recipes are in metric measurements.

Hopefully your scales will measure both metric and imperial but if you like to always work in one version, and convert from the other, here are the conversion tables for you to use. We have used American cup measures here, just in case you always wondered how to convert other recipes you may have into 'normal' measures. The first table is for volume/liquids and the second and third tables are for weight.

Conversion table for volume and liquids:

USA *Cups*	**Universal** *Tablespoons*	**Imperial** *Fluid oz*	**Imperial** *Pints*	**Metric** *ml*	**Other**
1/16	1			15	= 3 teasp
1/8	2	1		30	
¼	4	2	1/8	60	
½	8	4	¼	120	
¾	12	6	1/6	180	
1	16	8	½	240	
2	32	16	1	480	
4.2	68	34	2.1	1000	= 1 litre

Conversion table for weight (Imperial to Metric):

Imperial	Imperial	Metric	Metric
oz	lbs	g	kg
1	1/16	28	0.028
4	¼	113	0.113
8	½	227	0.227
16	1	454	0.454

Conversion table for weight (Metric to Imperial):

Metric	Metric	Imperial	Imperial
g	kg	oz	lbs
100	0.1	3.5	0.22
250	0.25	8.75	0.55
500	0.5	17.5	1.1
1000	1	35	2.2

Please note that:
1 teaspoon is approximately 5g of dry weight;
1 dessert spoon is approximately 10g of dry weight; and 1 tablespoon is approximately 15g of dry weight.
Please note that:
1 teaspoon is approximately 5ml of liquid;
1 dessert spoon is approximately 10ml of liquid; and
1 tablespoon is approximately 15ml of liquid.

Oven Temperature Conversions:

This table is the definitive oven conversion table. All of our recipes list Fahrenheit, centigrade and gas marks to cater for all kitchens. However, this may help you with other recipe books that you may have.

Fahrenheit	Centigrade	Gas mark	Description
225 – 275 f	110 – 135 c	0 – 1	Very Cool
300 – 325 f	150 – 165 c	2 – 3	Cool
350 – 375 f	175 – 190 c	4 – 5	Moderate
400 – 425 f	200 – 220 c	6 – 7	Hot
450 – 475 f	230 – 245 c	8 – 9	Very Hot

US/UK Food conversions:

This final table is for the different names of foods in the US and UK. We use the UK names in our recipes:

UK	US	UK	US
Aubergine	Eggplant	Mince	Ground meat
Biscuit	Cookie	Muesli	Granola
Chips	Fries	Porridge	Oatmeal
Coriander (herb)	Cilantro	Prawn	Shrimp
Courgette	Zucchini	Rocket (salad)	Arugula
Crisps	Chips	Sweets	Candy

Recipes

Recipe name: ____________________

Source: ____________________

Ingredients

Method

Notes

Recipes

Recipe name: ______________________________

Source: ______________________________

Ingredients

Method

Notes

Recipes

Recipe name: ______________________________

Source: ______________________________

Ingredients

Method

Notes

Recipes

Recipe name: ____________________

Source: ____________________

Ingredients

Method

Notes

Recipes

Recipe name: ____________________

Source: ____________________

Ingredients

Method

Notes

Recipes

Recipe name: ______________________________

Source: ______________________________

Ingredients

Method

Notes

Recipes

Recipe name: ______________________________

Source: ______________________________

Ingredients

Method

Notes

Recipes

Recipe name:

Source:

Ingredients

Method

Notes

Recipes

Recipe name: ______________________________

Source: ______________________________

Ingredients

Method

Notes

Recipes

Recipe name: ____________________

Source: ____________________

Ingredients

Method

Notes

Recipes

Recipe name: ______________________________

Source: ______________________________

Ingredients

Method

Notes

Recipes

Recipe name: ______

Source: ______

Ingredients

Method

Notes

Recipes

Recipe name: ______

Source: ______

Ingredients

Method

Notes

Recipes

Recipe name: __________

Source: __________

Ingredients

Method

Notes

For further information

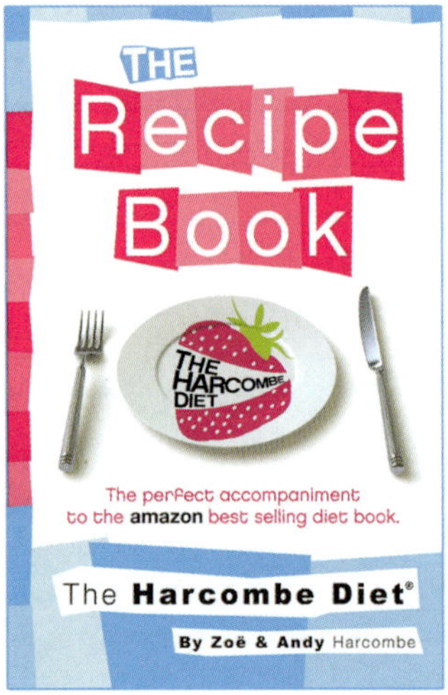

The Harcombe Diet:
The Recipe Book

Real food; great taste; optimal health – that's what The Harcombe Diet® is all about and here's how to do it. With over 100 recipes for Phase 1, another 100 for Phase 2 and some seriously special Phase 3 cheats, this is the ultimate diet-recipe book. If you want to eat well, lose weight and gain health – this is a must for your kitchen shelf.

ISBN 978-1-907797-07-1

The Harcombe Diet:
Stop Counting Calories
& Start Losing Weight

You've tried every diet under the sun. You've lost weight and put it back on. The more you diet, the more you crave food. You've given up hope of being slim. This book explains why. Count calories & end up a food addict. Stop Counting Calories & Start Losing Weight!

ISBN 978-1-907797-11-8

www.zoeharcombe.com
www.healthaspire.co.uk

Index